W9-BCK-930

STORY PATTERNS IN
GREEK TRAGEDY

RICHMOND LATTIMORE

Story Patterns
in Greek Tragedy

ANN ARBOR

THE UNIVERSITY OF MICHIGAN PRESS

FOREWORD

THIS book owes its origin to the invitation from University College of the University of London, to deliver the Lord Northcliffe Lectures, which were given there in May 1961. They are here printed substantially as they were given, with the addition of some notes. Translations used are my own, except where otherwise stated.

The visit to University College was a delightful period in my life, and it is a pleasure now to remember and record my gratitude to Sir Ifor Evans, Provost of University College, and Professor T. B. L. Webster for making it possible, and to them again and to many friends, new and old, in the academic community of London, for all they have done for me.

R.L.

CONTENTS

I

Tragedy as Story-Telling

WE still possess thirty-two tragedies by three Athenian poets. Individually, they are unlike each other, but together they form a group with a character of its own, different from all other poetry and drama. As a group, these tragedies are still extensively read and tolerably well understood, reread, studied, corrected sometimes to the point of torture, translated, acted, attended, interpreted, and argued about. I believe, though there is no proving it, that they are studied, even now, more extensively than any other dramatic corpus except the plays of Shakespeare. What is there about them that makes them what they are?

It seems that we have to keep on asking this. We seem, for our own satisfaction, to have to account for them, or try to. We do not know the reasons Aeschylus, Sophocles, and Euripides had for writing what they wrote. They do not, in the manner of Shaw, openly incorporate their own comments on their own dramas, by way of introduction, epilogue, or extensive stage directions. We may know some of their reasons. We know, for instance, that they were competing for prizes. It is not enough; a desire for an award will not account for *Agamemnon* or *Antigone*. There must always have been more, an intention and design. And we shall not know it, for any given play.

But this is also true. When the dramatist has produced or circulated his play, he no longer owns it. It is true of the meanest work of art. Once released, it is out there in the world, at the mercy of everyone. It is now a fact of nature: to be explained; so criticized; and so defined, since definition is the beginning of criticism.

We could start with the first great definer and systematic critic of tragedy from antiquity, Aristotle. But if we do, we shall never be ended. Aristotle's *Poetics* presents more problems of interpretation than most of the plays themselves. It will be more than enough if, sometimes, we arrive by our own roads at conclusions Aristotle once reached; or at least we think he did.

My first observation begins, however, with a paraphrase of Aristotle, who said that tragedy is the imitation of an action.[1] Rephrased, this means to me that it acts out a story, or, as we more often meet it, gives the story in a form that could be acted out. It is a kind of story-telling, whatever else it may be. We should add: a serious story, seriously told; in verse; to be presented, under a set of strict rules, in a dramatic competition at the public sacred festivals of Athens: and particularly at the one called the City Dionysia. Such, perhaps, are the minimal, indispensable characteristics of Athenian tragedy. Later, as we proceed, we may find more. Even these simple characteristics can generate a structure of themes so complex and varied that it is impossible at any time to be viewing the whole of it at once. As a result, some aspects, like the "tragical," are likely to be exaggerated; others, like the poetic, neglected. On another occasion I tried to isolate and study the poetic aspect;[2] this time, I should like to study the story-telling; always, I realize that we are falsely detaching what belongs together, for the poetry, the narrative, and all the other processes of drama are always, in a sense, one single process.

As is well known, the stories told in tragedies were not

pure fictions invented by the tragic poets. The material was drawn almost exclusively from the legends and myths which, in Homer, Hesiod, and their successors, or in oral tradition, constituted a sort of loose history of the Greek world from the beginnings to the Dorian conquest. Mostly, the general outlines of these stories were secure as given: details might vary considerably; in choosing his variants, or in shaping and weighting the unvariable, the poet made his plot. I shall call this given material the Legend.

I should like to illustrate this kind of material limitation, combined with material option or freedom, furnished from legend to the poet, by one main example. Oedipus is one of the popular heroes of tragedy, appearing as a major figure in perhaps a dozen tragedies by various poets, including Aeschylus, Sophocles, and Euripides, as a secondary figure in still others, we do not know how many. What story or stories did these poets have at their disposal? What did the Legend require, permit, forbid?[3]

Oedipus was king of Thebes. He solved, foiled, and abolished the Sphinx. He killed Laius, his father. He married his widowed mother, without knowing who she was; but the secrets of the family were discovered. He quarreled with his sons. All this, to the Greek of the fifth century, was "so," historical fact rather than myth, and certainly not fiction.

But we hear far more about Oedipus than this, and the further details give scope for variation. Sometimes we know some of the variants. We can proceed by asking questions. How could he marry his mother in ignorance? In Sophocles, because he was a foundling, set out to die because an oracle had predicted that he must kill his father and marry his mother, rescued by a pair of kind shepherds, and brought up by the king and queen of Corinth. He thought he was their son. Was the story always told thus? In one story the queen may have hidden the child from someone (her husband?) who was seeking him out (to murder him?).[4] In *Oedipus at Colonus* we meet him blind. Was he always blind at the end of his days? In *Oedipus Tyrannus* we hear how he blinded himself. Euripides had him blinded by the henchmen of Laius, so we know that this circumstance at least was free for variation.[5] Where did he meet his father? Near Potniae, says Aeschylus; near Daulis, says Sophocles; but both say, at a meeting of three ways; perhaps *that* is compulsory?[6] How did he kill his father and did he know who he was? No, says Sophocles, and describes the wayside brawl in which Oedipus killed or routed a whole party of servants. The same servants who, in Euripides, pinned him to the ground and blinded him? The stories do not seem to agree. What happened to Oedipus after his secrets came out? He went on ruling in Thebes, says Homer.[7] No, he did not, says Sophocles: so even Homer can be contradicted, on a detail at least: Creon, Iocasta's brother, took over, until Oedipus's sons grew up; Oedipus had to leave Thebes; as to just when, Sophocles himself is a little vague;[8] Euripides has him living at Thebes in retirement until the battle of Thebes fought by his sons.[9] For his sons were cursed by Oedipus and fought for the kingdom. Why cursed? Because they used the old man despitefully, that seems clear. And why did they fight for the kingdom? Because they were cursed (Aeschylus); because they were greedy and ambitious (Sophocles); because one of them was greedy and ambitious (Euripides).

We need not dwell on little details like the name of Oedipus's mother, Epicaste in Homer,[10] Iocasta in Athenian drama. Oedipus's place of burial is another vexed question with various answers.[11] And there are the supplementary

stories and their people. When and how did Antigone enter
the legend? Was she always engaged to Haemon, the son of
Creon, and when she tried to bury her brother and was condemned, did she die in the belief that Haemon had deserted
her? So Sophocles.[12] Or rather did Haemon secretly rescue
her, marry her, and did they have a son named Maeon? Thus,
it appears, Euripides told the story, with some support from
Homer.[13] Who first brought in Ismene, and was she the
gentle sister who did not dare defy Creon, or the amorous
one who was killed by Tydeus, on the orders of Athene
because she was caught making love with Periclymenus?[14]
And why did Tydeus and Athene care? Or, once more,
were both Antigone and Ismene burned to death by Laoda-
mas the son of Eteocles because they both buried the body of
Polyneices, and were caught?[15] We do find support in
ancient literature and art for all these variants, and more,
which seem so wild when we contemplate the *Antigone* of
Sophocles in all its monumental unity.

Sophocles then (it seems) could only make his play
through a series of choices, in which far more was rejected
than taken. With the adventures of these legendary persons
goes their character. What were they like? Sophocles, says
one ancient critic, "could characterize a whole person in a
little half-line or a single word."[16] It is an enlightening exag-
geration, an inspired half-truth. The characters of drama are
made partly, originally, by what they do and what happens
to them: the little details of what they say find their place in
the whole, and illuminate it. In all this, the tragic poet had
wide discretionary powers, and their responsibilities, misuse
of which would mean failure.

And last of all, perhaps: What of it? What is to be made
of the story? If we think again of Oedipus: What is the cause

of, or at least the reason in, this history, which is his down-fall? Ancestral guilt, the crimes and follies of Laius, or Laius and Iocasta together? Inner fault in Oedipus, pride, or head-long anger, or some vein of witlessness running in a keen mind? Simple punishment for too great success, the envy of the gods, or what modern scholars have chosen to call, mis-leadingly I think, *hybris* and *nemesis*?[17] Will the poet tell us what he thinks, or will he tell the story and leave us to piece out the meaning for ourselves—if there is any? He will very seldom tell us what he thinks. When he does, we are hardly ever sure of it. That is a part of the form of drama.

We have at this point gone rather beyond the material limits of tragedy, the facts so to speak which the poet may or must accept, or choose among. But between the realm of facts, and of their interpretation, there is no sharp line to be drawn. All these given legends have, despite their freedoms, certain sets of limitations, which I call the material limita-tions, and which I have described above. But drama is shaped also, it seems, by certain formal conditions or formal limitations as well, patterns of story as it were, less easy to define and illustrate. The story itself, as an ordered series of events, has its own rights.

If I may leave Greek tragedy for a moment: Portia had three caskets, gold, silver, lead. To win her beautiful and valuable hand, a suitor must choose the right one. She had three suitors: two proud princes, and a penniless scholar. The first prince tapped the golden casket, the second tapped the silver. Both were wrong. The scholar found Portia in the lead. That was all right. She had fallen in love with him anyway, and found it hard to keep from cheating.

The story has a logic proper to good story-telling, rather than a fidelity to the probabilities of real life. A real prince, given the first choice, could so easily have got Portia. Whether because he had brains enough to see that there was no point in hiding her except in the most unlikely place, or whether because her father had double-bluffed and put her in the gold after all—stupid or sharp, he could have carried her off, leaving us, the story's listeners, as frustrated as Bassanio. The story has a kind of moral rhetoric too—the virtues of humility, or all that glisters is not gold—but it is not quite the kind of morals applicable to real people; for after all, Bassanio, however generous, is just a fortune-hunter who is going to live on Portia's unearned increment and never do another lick of work the rest of his life. These questions, of story-life and real life, will concern us a little later; what concerns us here is just what we may call *the rights of the story.* The order of events is essential. The moral order goes with it. It is just as important for Bassanio to choose last as it is for him to choose right.

Add this: when the details of the story do so cohere, we feel a sense of necessity, of must-be-so: one could almost call it fate.

Briefly, let me apply this notion of right order to a few tragic stories, or types of story. Eteocles chose six champions, himself the seventh, to defend the seven gates of Thebes. These gates were to be attacked by seven enemy champions; the seventh was Polyneices, his estranged brother. The beauty of the construction is wrecked unless these two are chosen to fight each other. More: they must be chosen last, or else the stringing out of comparatively disinterested champions, six against six, is dreary anticlimax. But if when, say, the third or fourth champion is named, Eteocles said "I will fight him," that is worse than anticlimax, it is monstrous. If not thus, then so. When we reach the climax, the matching of the brothers, we feel: this had to be.

And this is the moment of truth or revelation or recognition when the hero in drama sees the shape of the action in which he is involved. So Eteocles, when he sees that Polyneices is the seventh man and he is the seventh defender (*Seven Against Thebes*, 654–6):

> O great abomination, hatred of the gods,
> o house of sorrows, seed of Oedipus, my own,
> here are my father's curses. They are coming true.

It is right, says Eteocles, that I should fight him, τίς ἄλλος μᾶλλον ἐνδικώτερος (673). The chorus protests, he can still change his plans, but Eteocles is driven by the shape of his story (686–97):

> What is this madness, child? Let not the frenzy swell
> to burst your heart, the spear's desperate fury drive you.
> Cast off this evil passion.

> No, since the god strongly hastens this action on,
> let the whole seed of Oedipus, that Phoebus hates,
> run down the storm on waves of death, and take its fate.

> The fierce teeth of desire are in you. It drives
> you to complete this killing, and win a bitter yield
> of blood that is taboo.

> Yes, for the black abominable father's curse
> has settled now on my dry eyes that will not weep
> and speaks of profit won before the death to be.

The curse the fate the action and the choice all coincide.

We may see the rights of the story equally well in quite another kind of action. Consider the story of the foundling, or we might call him exposeling, the unwanted or dangerous baby who is left in the wilderness to die, but is rescued and recognized. The story appears again and again, in history of sorts (Cyrus, Romulus), in fairy story (Snow White), in later romance (*The Winter's Tale*), again and again in Menander and the Latin comic poets.[18] It was used, with ironical inversions, by Sophocles in *Oedipus Tyrannus*, and told straight with a happy ending in the lost *Tyro*,[19] and probably *Alexander*,[20] also lost. Euripides used it in *Ion*, and in numerous lost plays.[21] I will not dwell yet on the variations of the story, except to say this: Children who are unwanted have often been exposed in actual fact. Sometimes somewhere probably they still are. They have seldom survived. But in story-telling, the child exposed is the child saved; he, or she, always survives. If he is not to survive, there is really no point, no *dramatic* point, in having him exposed at all. But he is thought to have died, and the recognition of his identity is regularly the climax of the story, its moment of truth.

The foundling theme is not, indeed, the only pattern for the story of the missing child. The child may not be exposed at all, but stolen away by one deceit or another, or by simple flight. Thus Zeus himself from Kronos[22] or the Christ-child from Herod,[23] and thus Orestes from Aegisthus,[24] Cresphontes from Polyphontes.[25] He may be thought to have died; if not, he must at least be misidentified. Nor, after all, does the missing person have to be a baby: the lost baby is just one popular variant in the general pattern of the missing person, whose "lost" status leads to mistaken identity and its resulting complications of action and situation: Odysseus thought to be far away and probably dead, unrecognized among the suitors in his own house and under his wife's nose; Menelaus thought dead by Helen the moment before he arrives to repossess her;[26] Orestes and Iphigeneia, each (like Sebastian and Viola) thinking the other is dead;[27] Iphigeneia about to take her part in the slaughter of Orestes, not knowing who he is;[28] Merope on the point of killing her long-lost son, Cresphontes, in the belief he is that son's murderer;[29] Creusa attempting to murder her son, Ion, believing him to be her husband's bastard when he is, in fact, her own;[30] Telegonus actually killing his father (Odysseus), whom he had set out to reclaim.[31] In fact, mistaken identity is so powerful a matrix to generate dramatic and melodramatic situations that Aristotle has made it an essential element of tragedy: for Professor Else has demonstrated with I think complete and sensational success that the famous Aristotelian *hamartia* can mean neither fault, or flaw, in character, nor yet an error in judgment, but simply a mistake about the identity of a person.[32]

We add, however, that a mistake about identity in this narrower sense is not the only kind of mistake that can be made about a person. His character, which often means what he has done, can be mistaken: the slandered but pure young man, Joseph, Hippolytus, Bellerophon, or the pure young woman, Desdemona, Imogen, Hero; these, too, are in a sense mistaken identities: *King Lear* works in sets of them, true-false, good-bad. In either kind of sequence, the shape of the story asserts itself. The mistaken person may or may not be rescued, but the mistaken truth must be. After the *hamartia,* of whatever sort, recognition is likely to follow. For the person deceived: not us, the readers, the audience. Usually, *we* know.

> As flies to wanton boys are we to the gods.
> They kill us for their sport.

That is a dramatic person speaking, his "we": we, the audience, are raised to the level of gods, or wanton boys, by the story-teller, who kills his people for our sport.[33] But their error must be resolved, and they must end on our level; at least (a major proviso) as far as the main action is concerned.[34]

We have had a glimpse of certain story-patterns, their rights and rules. They operate not only in tragedy, but in myths or *fabulae sacrae,* fairy-stories, and some of the more naive narrations in history. This does not mean that tragedy *is,* or is made out of, *fabula sacra,*[35] fairy-story, or history: rather that all, insofar as they are stories, will obey the rules and exhibit the shapes of story-telling.

But tragedy is more than story-telling: that is essential to it, but does not exhaust its meaning, nor adequately account for its nature. Where Aristotle leaves his critics dissatisfied is precisely at this point. Why, for all he says, is a well-made play not the ultimate in drama? Why are Menander, Scribe, Oscar Wilde, Moss Hart and Noel Coward not superior to Aeschylus and Shakespeare?

Let me try to illustrate, by means of a drastic example, the difference between a good story and a tragic action. Consider for a moment a folk tale from the modern Greek, called "The Effendi of the Chickpeas."[36] A tramp found a chickpea in the road, figured that if he planted it he'd have a quart of chickpeas, if he planted them again there would be a bushel, and so on, until he reached ten thousand bushels. What would he do with all that? He went to the king and asked him for the loan of his store-houses. The king thought, "He must be very rich, I'll give him my daughter." But first he tested him. He gave him a hard bed to sleep on. The tramp happened to lose his chickpea, which rolled under his spine and he couldn't sleep a wink. Next night it was a soft bed. But he found the pea and put it in his pocket and slept. So he passed as a true tender nobleman, and married the princess, and she with her numerous bridal escort went on their way, with the tramp going on ahead wondering where he was going to put his bride and all these people, because he had no house at all. But on his way he fell in with a dragon. The dragon said yes, he had a palace and gold and silver and food and dishes and servants, and the tramp could have them; but at the end of a year, he will return, and ask the tramp some riddles, and if he can't answer, the tramp will be devoured. Forty days and nights the tramp (or effendi) entertained the party, and then lived blissfully for a year, until the dragon was due to return. Terror. But a little old man knocked at the door and was admitted, and answered all the riddles. The dragon's last question was: "What happens to me now?" "Oh, you break in two, and half of you will be a golden lintel, and the other half will be a silver threshold." Then the little old man vanished, and the Effendi of the Chickpeas woke up in the morning and found the lintel and the threshold, and he and his wife lived happily ever after.[37]

Perhaps this little *paramythion,* as the Greeks would call it, seems too blatantly untragic, or even undramatic, to be worth talking about in connection with such matters as we are here discussing. Yet it does not lack *all* the elements of the proper tragical story. This story does have a kind of inevitability ("fate"), controlled by its shape and expressed in story-patterns ("The Princess and the Pea,")[38] "Rumpel-stiltskin"); the tramp-effendi, once launched on his career, *must* succeed, the dragon *must* be foiled. That the story is told, not mimed or acted-out, is inessential here. It could easily be made into a one-act play or a dramatic ballet or mime. It has a happy ending. So, we must keep reminding ourselves, did many plays called tragedies;[39] and if we say that a tragic story can only come out right after trial by suffering and fear, what could be more terrible than the prospect of being eaten by a dragon? If the dragon is preposterous, a childish bugaboo, so was the Sphinx of Thebes, who also sang riddles at you and ate you, or something, if you failed to answer.[40] The lived-happily-ever-after ending, in a bliss which would be truly boring, because the blissful couple will never *do* anything more except eat and drink and have babies, may be unrealistic; but Orwell complained of the same thing in Dickens.[41] Dickens is surely a serious writer of fiction.

The real differences lie perhaps not in what is there but in what is missing. The whole tone lacks seriousness, but how? For one thing, the tale is told, as we have it—as we should have to have it—in a simple story-teller's *demotike* or vernacular lacking the imagery and the rhetoric and the rhythmic line which go so far to make tragedy what it is. Greek Tragedy is poetry. That is absolutely vital. I have pursued that issue elsewhere,[42] or tried to, and shall not do so here, for there are other issues. There is the airy idiocy of the original plot: it reminds us of the bright ideas of Aristophanes' bumpkin-heroes, like storming heaven on a dung-beetle;[43] it inverts the moral fable—as comedy often inverts —of "counting your chickens before they are hatched." It is true that the plot rests on mistaken identity, and so may tragedy. It may mean something that the truth is not revealed; perhaps there is no truth then, no falsehood; in

fairy-story's wishful world, perhaps the tramp can turn out
to *be* an effendi, after all. It is not out of character. For there
is no character. Possibly, there lies the essential difference.[44]
The tramp arises through dumb luck; or by that unmoti-
vated presence—who, we admit, also appears in epic and
tragedy—the *deus ex machina* or fairy godmother. Yet that,
again, is of the essence of the pure fairy-tale. In tragedy or
in epic the superhuman aid is not often merely handed out
as it is to the effendi. Odysseus has his Athene, but she helps
one who is so like her;[45] and even so, throughout and in the
end Odysseus acts and chooses for himself. The effendi has
no character, makes no dramatic choices, and his story has
no motivation. So no morality. And so at last no reality,
none of that more-real-than-real illusion of reality that the
dramatic abstraction spells us into, where we suspend belief
and find the stories of Orestes, Oedipus, and Hippolytus,
in their imagined time, as real as actual histories of actual
people; and come out impressed, horrified, moved or
shaken, not merely amused.[46]

We now find ourselves, perhaps, clutching a bundle of
elements, characteristics, features of tragedy. It is hard to
know what to call them without being disastrously misled
by our own terms. Aristotle, for instance, speaks of the
lyrical element as ἡδυσμα,[47] literally a "sweetening" of the
drama. But lyric poetry is not jam on the bread or sugar on
the yoghurt. Or, I had almost said, it should not be: "should"
is a deadly trap, which leads the critic to make his pattern
and then squeeze extant tragedy into it; or else to ignore the
facts.

Facts are what we are after. And here are some facts about
Athenian tragedy as we know it. It works with the materials
of Legend, part fixed, part fluid. It is guided in part by the

shape of the story which is being enacted. It has the form of a highly stylized structure of poetry and rhetoric, and uses characters abstracted from the personalities of flesh-and-blood life, offering them, as it seems, for judgments other than what we would pass on real people. Despite such artificiality, it frequently compels us to a conviction and feeling at least as deep as what we would feel about real people; in order to do this, we have to suspend judgment and make concessions, but tragedy makes us make them, and makes us forget that we have made them. It projects a world of people who are fictitious, but not a fairy-story world, because these people and their stories are represented as deeply involved in personal and moral issues. When such conviction is complete, and the persons, and what they say, and the progress of the story closely cohere, we feel a sense of inevitability and rightness sometimes more pure than we feel when presented with an account of actual events.

We must add: sometimes the tragic poets fail to do all this; when they do, critics have been quick to notice and complain, and other critics to apologize and defend, or rationalize.

I have spoken of the moral dimension, and this brings up an issue which must be a little bit cleared (but briefly, because this is not my chief concern here). Does a play always, does it ever, have a moral?[48] What is the relation of the moral to the dramatic action? Did the Athenian dramatic poet ever, or always, write to justify—or *un*justify—the ways of God to men? He has been called primarily a prophet, or a teacher of his people.[49] Is this right?

First, truly, we cannot recover *intentions*; we can only, once again, observe results, or facts.

It is true that the Greek moralizes incessantly. It is true

that the tragic poet sometimes seems to be propounding a moral, counter-dramatically, in his own person rather than that of his character or, more frequently, Chorus.[50] It is also true that at or near the end of the play, he frequently gives us a few lines that do comment on, and seem meant to summarize, the action as a whole.[51]

The whole question is enormous, and I do not know that it has been adequately studied. I cannot do it any justice here. I will say, briefly, that I do not know of any compendious author's-moral which completely sums up the action. Or rather, I should say, I do know one, from *Philoctetes,* which will be discussed later on.[52]

Elsewhere, we find author's-morals which are fragmentary, one-sided, and occasionally indigestible. I must limit myself to just two examples. Take the concluding lines of *Antigone,* spoken by the Chorus:

> Toward a happy life, to be thoughtful
> is the first need. One must do the gods
> no impiety. Claims made too great
> bring down great blows on those who have claimed
> too much in their pride,
> and at last, in old age, teach wisdom.

If we are ever sure, we can be sure that this is Sophocles speaking, and speaking as we are usually taught to expect him to: this is orthodox, and highly respectable. Note, however: because this is Sophocles' view here, we are not to demand that he hold it all through his seventy years of dramatic composition: and note again that the moral applies strictly to the *last part* of the action, the tragedy of Creon, having little bearing on the tragic choice and suffering of Antigone, for Antigone did the gods no impiety, and she died forlorn: and note finally that it has little meaning at all except as a grace note on the story which has in detail been enacted.

At the end of *The Eumenides,* Aeschylus makes Athene and the appeased goddesses exchange prayers and blessings for the peace and prosperity of Athens. I have said that one cannot judge intentions, but for this passage those who hold that Aeschylus assumed the part of a public spokesman—a prophet if you must insist, speaking to his people—are almost surely right. But this is done after the play is over, the last of the human actors has left the stage. Aeschylus has contrived that his concluding pageant shall have grown, by well-connected stages, scene by scene, from the opening lines of the trilogy. And yet, if we push the civic morals of the close back into *Agamemnon,* they will be found to have only the vaguest kind of application.

It is hard, I think impossible, to interpret a whole tragedy in terms of one moral proposition. Look for the moral dimension. The patterns of dramatic story themselves, to which I shall return are of moral construction, and have their own moral materials.

II

Patterns of Tragic Narrative: Hamartia, Pride, Choice

T HERE is no one pattern, whether of action or of moral, which constitutes *the* pattern of tragedy.

There are numerous patterns of action or tragic themes. Most, but not all of them have moral dimensions.

The presence of one such theme does not preclude the use of others.

The themes I name are identified by observation, and are not to be thought of as master-themes acknowledged and deliberately used by Greek authors.

Hamartia or The Tragic Flaw

We start with the pattern which is perhaps the most familiar of all, and is thought of by many as the master-pattern for the interpretation of all Greek tragedy. In terms of story, we may take it as the story of the downfall of a good or noble person through some flaw in his character: such as pride, impiety, overconfidence, ambition, anger.

The popularity of this pattern is partly due to the belief that it is authorized in a passage from Aristotle's *Poetics*,[1] which will be tentatively rendered thus: "Such a man (i.e., the best tragic hero) is one who is not preeminent for goodness and justice, but who does not suffer misfortune through wickedness or worthlessness, but through some *hamartia*." This *hamartia* has been most popularly supposed to mean "flaw," that is, of character. From a consideration of the cases where the term is actually used in tragedy, I would conclude independently that the word in this form cannot signify a permanent characteristic in a person, pride, quickness to anger, etc., but must refer to a mistaken or wrong act or to a mistake that has been made;[2] but in any case, as I have mentioned before, Else has shown that Aristotle, in his context, must be talking about something much more narrow and specific, namely, the misidentification of a person.[3]

If this is indeed true, the Aristotelian sanction for the *hamartia* pattern—at least as derived from this passage— vanishes. That does not mean that the *hamartia* pattern must vanish too. For, first, when we interpret tragedy through Aristotle, we have to interpret Aristotle first: though the problems are related, they are by no means identical. And, second, Aristotle does, elsewhere, seem to commend Homer for making Achilles a good man but choleric and stubborn (which plainly he is).[4] Finally, with or without Aristotelian authority, the pattern of the tragic flaw deserves to be considered on its own merits. Do we, in fact, find it in the tragedies themselves? I do not mean, are the dramatic persons understood to have flaws? Of course, they do. They are people, or human heroes, not angels; even when divine, seen in action as human, and not angelic (only secondary characters, perhaps, can be perfect?). But is there a dynamic flaw which operates the story and gives it shape?

Such cases are hard to name. I find, of the thirty-two extant plays, fifteen in which the Tragic Fault has little or nothing to do with the main action,[5] and ten more where one could establish it as a major theme only by straining the dramatic facts.[6] The group of fifteen includes the plays with happy endings, like *Iphigeneia in Tauris,* the parts of trilogies which end with reconciliation or with the issue unresolved, the plays with multiple plots, like *Andromache* and *The Phoenician Women,* and the revenge plays, where the effects of anger or vindictiveness seem to be absorbed into a quite different pattern, to be discussed later.[7]

Next, there is an interesting group of four plays by Sophocles in which the flaw, wrongness, or *hamartia* seems to be specifically mentioned by the author, yet cannot, after careful consideration, be seen as the major motive. The best case is *Ajax*. By proudly rejecting the proffered help of Athene, Ajax earned her hatred. The arms of Achilles were awarded by the Achaeans to Odysseus, and Ajax, furious, set out to slaughter his enemies (once his friends) but Athene drove him mad and turned his onslaught against the cattle and herdsmen. He recovered his senses, knew himself disgraced and threatened with ignominious death, and found nothing left him but suicide. So told, with the dimensions of detail disregarded, his story reads like that of a great man destroyed by the flaw of pride. Sophocles even seems to say this at one point, where the messenger reports what Calchas said about Ajax:

> For those oversized and insensate bulks of men
> go down heavily in disasters the gods contrive.
> So spoke the prophet; such a one, grown great in man's
> stature, then thinks of himself as something more
>   than man.[8]

And yet, this pattern of fault or pride and fall does not work all the way to the end. For Ajax in his death scene is not punished, but vindicated. He sets himself a test (*peira*) and passes it,[9] and attains his salvation.[10] He leaves life on his own terms, keeps his pride, and at the end his chief enemy,

Odysseus, acknowledges his greatness. Can such pride be called a fault at all when it empowers a hero to outlast, and somehow put to shame, the vindictiveness of even Athene?

In *Antigone,* again, the Chorus charges the heroine with the fault of stubbornness.[11] She is stubborn. It does destroy her, of course, but it is not in the whole view seen as weakness, fault, or flaw. Few, certainly, will argue that this is meant to be Antigone's inner weakness which destroys her. In *Philoctetes,* Neoptolemus justly charges Philoctetes with stubbornness which will ruin not only Philoctetes but Neoptolemus too.[12] But Philoctetes finally is made to relent, and disaster is averted. In *Oedipus at Colonus* Creon charges Oedipus with irascibility, which always clouds his character.[13] Creon is a hostile witness, but the charge is true. Antigone, in fact, says the same thing.[14] Oedipus keeps his anger. It brings down his enemies, not himself. He goes out as a great hero, unrepentant, just after cursing his sons.

We are left with three cases where it is possible to apply the Tragic Fault all the way. In *The Persians,* Aeschylus plainly means that Xerxes ruined himself and his country through pride, greed, ambition, and violence. It is only hard to make such a list of qualities into a *fault* in character; for this play, they constitute all the character Xerxes has; at least until he failed; and we do not see or hear him until he has failed. In *Oedipus Tyrannus,* we certainly have a noble nature flawed by the anger and impatience of the tyrant; but this does not completely account for the structure of interlocking events that makes his story. In *Hippolytus,* Euripides shows the flaw of self-satisfaction and pedantry in the young hero, but I am not sure he means to. He could equally well be trying—as Sophocles may be in *Ajax*—to show a man too good for the world he lives in; and what

the world does to such a man. The tragic-flaw theory may
be applied to these plays, but it is not, surely, all-sufficient.

Is it ever, and have I been attacking a position conceded
to be untenable? Yet I do know one tragedy in which the
pattern of the tragic flaw is classically seen, a master-pattern
practically all-sufficient. It is not a Greek tragedy, but
Shakespeare's *Coriolanus*; here pride, contempt for his fellow
man, is the sole and sufficient cause of the great man's
downfall. *Coriolanus* is the model for the theory; but not
one Greek tragedy approaches the model.

Pride and Punishment

(*Achilles to Priam.*) Now let us remember our dinner.
For even fair-haired Niobe was mindful of eating,
although her twelve children had been destroyed in her palace,
six daughters, and six sons in the strength of their young
    manhood.
Apollo with his silver bow killed the boys, angered
with Niobe, and the daughters Artemis of the showering
    arrows
killed, because Niobe likened herself to fair-faced Leto.
She said Leto had borne two, but she herself had borne many,
and the two, though they were only two, destroyed all her
    children.[15]

Great indignation (νέμεσις) on the part of God overtook
Croesus because, one may suppose, he considered himself to be
the happiest of all men.[16]

Since pride is a fault of character, there has been a natural
confusion between this theme and that of the tragic flaw.
The latter, however, is best seen as the weakness within an
otherwise strong structure, working from within, and with-

out necessarily implicating divine action: the former directly opposes man and god, or gods. The hero may challenge, affront, or even contend with the god, or he may like Croesus only feel offensively satisfied with himself. His story, or that of Niobe, will stand at one pole: the story of Coriolanus, entirely secular and developed through the dealings of men with men, at the other. The histories of Xerxes and Hippolytus stand somewhere between.

The story of pride and punishment is a rare but discernible pattern in tragedy. It has been claimed that the Greeks knew and described such punishable pride in its pattern by the master-name *hybris,* and this claim has been made so widely and, I think, so mistakenly, that I feel it is necessary to digress briefly on the meanings and nonmeanings of the word.

Hybris,[17] with its family of nouns, verbs, and adjectives, simple or compounded, may signify assault and battery,[18] rape,[19] foul play,[20] or plain physical disaster without motivation;[21] the activity of wild animal spirits,[22] rapacity and greed,[23] sexual lust;[24] in general, violence;[25] violent or *criminal* behavior;[26] thus insolence as in Milton's "Sons of Belial flown with insolence and wine";[27] bullying, the abuse of superior strength to humiliate the helpless living or outrage the helpless dead;[28] or the mockery of the sorrowful;[29] conversely, mutiny or rebelliousness in an inferior toward a superior;[30] and so, rather rarely, ordinary insolence.[31]

That the gods resent and punish such misbehavior is, undoubtedly, a firm Greek belief, but the term *hybris* is not regularly applied to the human member of the pride and punishment pattern: that is, it is not applied to Niobe,[32] to Ajax scorning Athene,[33] to Ajax Oileus (in *The Odyssey*) defying Athene and Poseidon,[34] to Thamyris (in Homer at least) contending with the Muses,[35] to Eurytus challenging Apollo,[36] Hippolytus refusing to worship Aphrodite,[37] the daughters of Proetus boasting that their father was richer than Hera.[38] This may mean, as a rare enlightened critic has hinted,[39] that men are not normally in a position to commit *hybris* against the gods. *Hybris* is indeed charged to Xerxes, but Xerxes had actually spoiled the shape of the world by hewing in two what God had made one and binding into one what God had made two, and in destroying the temples of the gods.[40] Plainly, *hybris* requires a violence more effective than pride, or mere arrogance of opinion.[41] Herodotus does not, of course, apply it to Croesus; his haunting and delusive spirit was not this, but *elpis*, hope, the staff and comfort of the weak, but the perilous siren who deceives the strong.[42]

But though *hybris* was not Croesus' offence, he did offend, and the *nemesis* of God overtook him.[43] In its construction and context, one is tempted to translate *nemesis* here into something like "retribution." But this sense is not supported in early Greek, for *nemesis* means, not an action or activity, or agency or agent, but a feeling; the feeling of shock, outrage, indignation at *hybris* or any other misbehavior.[44] This feeling is attributed to individuals and groups of human beings,[45] to the gods,[46] and to the dead, who require placation and are resentful when not placated.[47] As such, she is personified, a goddess with a cult, plus some puzzling biographical details; as, for instance, that bashful goose who fled from the embraces of the amorous swan, who was of course Zeus, but ultimately delivered the egg from which were hatched Helen and her brothers.[48] To call her the goddess of retribution is unwarranted; it requires a leap of inference—equating anger, a feeling, with punishment, an event, which may be the consequence of that feeling;[49] and such modern phrases as "to meet one's nemesis"—as if *nemesis* were a kind of personified Waterloo or impersonal Wellington—remain without any certain counterpart in ancient Greek.[50] The closest we get is perhaps in the story told by Pausanias, that Datis and the Medes when they arrived at Marathon brought with them a block of Parian marble for a *tropaion* to commemorate the battle they proposed to win. Pheidias made of this block the statue of *Nemesis* at Rhamnus.[51] This will fit, but does not require, the modern interpretation.

As in the case of *nemesis,* so even more with *hybris,* the belief has somehow grown up that this is a special semi-technical term devised by the Greeks to indicate that peculiar situation of human pride or challenge to divinity which is a unique taboo of Greek religion and whose under-standing is the sole key to Attic tragedy. Herein lies the modern error. I do not know where it came from, but certainly not from Aristotle or any other ancient critic of tragedy, for these offer no authority. Plainly, *hybris* is *not* a technical term (except in law, where it indicates physical violence) but a maid-of-all-work term for any kind of violence or insolence.[52]

Yet, to return; after the confusions and misnomers are cleared away, we are still left with a residue, the pattern of pride and punishment. It is a pattern-story, all too simple: as surely as the lost baby must be found, the proud challenger of the gods must be brought low.

Such an unmodified pattern has not—if we except *The Persians*—been followed in any surviving plays.[53] The titles of several lost tragedies, *Niobe*, by Aeschylus, and by

Sophocles, *Thamyras* by Sophocles, and possibly *Ajax Locrius* by Sophocles, suggest such plots.[54] Aristotle remarked, rather strangely, that the whole story of *Niobe* was too long for a single tragedy;[55] Aristophanes, more understandably, seems to indicate that it was too short, for he complained that the action dragged.[56] The theme, too simple, tends in practice to be complicated into something else; or reduced to a subtheme, as analogue.

For if a god, jealous of power and honor, simply uses his superior strength to crush the offender, what is that but *hybris,* in the important sense of power abused or plain bullying? So indeed, when jealous Hera destroyed her rival, Semele, that is called *hybris,*[57] and it is *hybris* again when Aphrodite tramples on her challengers.[58] Stories of pride and punishment are often alluded to in passing, a by-theme for mere pathos, as in Achilles' allusion to Niobe, or briefly to point a moral for action to men. The theme is applied to Agamemnon, but does not tell his story.[59] Told exclusively from and for man's point of view, the warnings against pride, presumption, challenge, are salutary and proper. The god appears as, indeed, *nemesis* in our English sense, the punitive morality. But when the story is spelled out at length, and the divine antagonist takes his place as a full-scale character in a story, he loses his moral invulnerability. We fall into the pattern of the revenge story, where, regularly, the righteous grievance of the avenger is lost sight of in the cruelty of the vengeance.[60] For it is difficult to make a person suffer before our eyes without generating sympathy for the sufferer; and if the cause of the suffering is a person, however august or holy, or divine, there is danger of revulsion.

Perhaps this, perhaps also an inherent oversimplicity,

lack of capacity for dramatic complication, is the reason why pride-and-punishment is a pattern rarely found as a tragic plot, though common in allusive moralizing and as a by-theme. Often, it is an afterthought: to account for events: so, in the form of failure to worship, the material cause that sets off a chain of disasters: Aphrodite forgotten, the sins of Helen and Clytaemestra, the Trojan War:[61] Artemis forgotten, and the Calydonian Boar[62] or, one might add, the cross fairy forgotten, and the princess put to sleep. Or we find justification of the god's anger in violent resistance to cult by Lycurgus or Pentheus,[63] a more serious offence than mere pride in beauty or skills. Even here, there is danger; at the end of *The Bacchae* Dionysus has seemed brutal and childish; humanwise, he tries to defend himself, and only makes his case sound worse.[64] That is Euripides; but we have a fragment from the lost *Niobe* of Aeschylus, in which the heroine herself comments on her fate:

> God plants the cause in men
> when he desires utterly to ruin a whole house.
> Meanwhile, he who is only mortal should take care
> of the prosperity that comes from God, nor speak
> too bold.[65]

The tone is majestic, but uneasy. The poet tries simultaneously to defend the rightness and the omnipotence of God while still feeling—despite the loaded dice—that the story of a conflict in which a human being takes part requires some element of human responsibility—that is, choice. Plato, whose objection to these very lines by Aeschylus was for a long time their attestation,[66] offered his own solution in "the announcement of Necessity (Anangke), the daughter of Lachesis." The souls, about to begin a new life, shall choose their lives. These lives, once chosen, shall then proceed on a compulsory course. But the original choice is the person's: virtue is the slave of no master, and they may have virtue as they prefer it. "The responsibility is the chooser's; the god is not responsible."[67] Plato's pronouncement is, of course, arbitrary, and rests on one of his myths or parables; philosophers have not solved this problem. But the unsolved problem itself offers a dramatic problem: the choice, or the illusion of choice, and its consequences.

The Patterns of Choice

Candaules, king of Lydia, was obsessed with the idea of proving that his wife was the most beautiful of women. He insisted that Gyges, his best friend, must hide in the bedroom and observe her when she was naked. Gyges objected, but he could not, one supposes, continue to resist the king; he finally obeyed. But the queen saw him. She said nothing to Candaules, but she sent for Gyges. "Now, Gyges, two roads lie before you; follow which one you wish; I give you your choice." There must be only one man alive who has seen her thus; Gyges must kill Candaules and marry her; or die himself. Gyges objected once more, but was forced to choose; he chose life.[68] From this moment of choice, or series of choices, Herodotus derives the fortunes of the house of Gyges, that is, the history of Lydia down through Croesus, as necessary consequence; or, conversely, the story demanded this series of actions and crucial choice; "it had to come out badly for Candaules."[69]

The storyteller in Herodotus has made him select and dramatize, often with full novelistic detail,[70] these moments of decision on which the course of history depends. So

again, before Marathon, Miltiades approached the Athenian
commander and laid before him the choice of two strate-
gies: "On you, Callimachus, depends the slavery or freedom
of Athens."[71] And so again Themistocles, before Salamis,
presented the Spartan commander-in-chief with a choice
between two courses of action.[72] In view of the frequency
of such patterns,[73] the historical critic may well feel cautious.
It is the moment of choice as a shape of action that concerns
us here. The shape is clearly seen in Prodicus's fable of
Heracles, who, at the outset of his career, came to a fork in
the road. The two ways, between which he must choose,
were represented each by a female spirit; one road and its
spirit offered a life of ease and pleasure, without achieve-
ment; the other, hardship, and greatness; he chose the latter,
else, one supposes, the world would have lacked its greatest
hero.[74] The shape of the forking of the ways forces a
choice.

"What shall I do?" said Orestes to Pylades. This moment
of choice, says Professor Rivier,[75] when the hero says "What
shall I do?" and realizes that he must make "une decision
capitale, souvent mortelle, toujours irrevocable," characterizes the archetype of all the situations in which Attic
drama, from Aeschylus on, placed its heroes. It seems convincing. We can indeed sometimes isolate a line or two
where such a major choice is made. It comes in *The Seven
Against Thebes,* just after Eteocles has realized where the
pattern of the seven gates and the seven combats has placed
him: the seventh man against the seventh enemy, his
brother. He accepts:

> I will go and stand against him
> myself. Who has a better right than I?[76]

It comes in *Iphigeneia in Aulis,* when Agamemnon has revoked and disowned his decision to sacrifice his daughter,
when Achilles is willing to fight alone against the Achaean
army to save her, and the whole expedition is likely to blow
up in civil war, and complete disorder. Iphigeneia has
pleaded all through for her life. Now she speaks:

> I have made my own decision. I will die. It is my wish
> that it shall be done with honor.[77]

It comes when the fate of Orestes is being decided, by the
judgment of twelve Athenian jurors, and the casting vote of
Athene in case of a tie; first when Athene announces, in
advance, how she will vote if it is necessary:

> This is a ballot for Orestes I shall cast.[78]

Then again, when the decision of the jurors is announced:

> The man before us has escaped the charge of blood.
> The ballots are in equal number for each side.[79]

Or again, the choice may be made, not *ab initio,* but as a
refusal to abandon a choice already made. We have noticed,
briefly, Orestes' "What shall I do?" The sequence in *Choe-
phori* runs:

ORESTES: What shall I do, Pylades? Be shamed to kill my
    mother?
PYLADES: What then becomes thereafter of the oracles
    declared by Loxias at Pytho? What of sworn oaths?
    Count all men hateful to you rather than the gods.
ORESTES: I judge that you win. Your advice is good.[80]

We do not hear Orestes make his original choice. It was
made before the play began. At the point of action, he

flinched, then remade his decision. In other plays, such as *Prometheus, Antigone, Philoctetes,* we may find a whole series of efforts to dislodge a person from a position already assumed.

While, therefore, it would be easy to construct a formula according to which circumstances combine and force the hero to make one terrible, difficult, decisive, positive choice which determines the ensuing trend of the action, such a formula would be too simple to contain the facts of Greek drama as we find them.

Antigone, for example, might be considered the drama of choice *par excellence,* yet the master-choice, which springs the whole action, Antigone's decision to bury Polyneices, is enacted indirectly, through the refusal of Ismene to share it.[81] Antigone has assumed that she must do this. We never hear her cry: "What shall I do?" The choice is also given in retrospect when Ismene tries to change her mind:

> You chose to live: I chose to die.[82]

The choice of Ajax is death, in a manner and circumstance which shall be directed by himself. But the decision is not thus plainly given, but in general terms:

> I must seek out some test
> with the result that I shall show my aged father
> that the son he sired was no heartless coward.[83]

On his next appearance, at the close of a long speech, he indicates that he has found the way to carry out the decision he had made:

> For I am going to that place where I must go.
> Do as I tell you, and perhaps you yet will hear
> that I, who am so vexed, have found deliverance.[84]

The next time he appears, it will be with his sword, alone, to die. He has set the scene up; but the plot, Sophocles' purpose to enact his death scene before our eyes, has made deception necessary, and the language is cryptic.[85]

Dramatic deception, then, may preclude the kind of forthright decision between clear alternatives which we began by considering. In *The Women of Trachis* the crucial choice is Deianeira's decision to send the shirt of Nessus to Heracles, her husband. Here are the circumstances. Heracles is about to come home after a long absence. He has sent home a beautiful captive, to whom he has already made love, with the intention of maintaining her in the house as a second wife. Deianeira has secretly kept the shirt given her by the centaur Nessus, stained with the centaur's life-blood and the Hydra's poison. He told her it was love-magic:

> it is a charm
> for Heracles' heart, so that he shall never look
> on another woman, and love her more than you.

Shall Deianeira use it, or submit to defeat by a younger rival? She debates it with her confidantes, the chorus—inexperienced women younger than she:[86]

DEIANEIRA: I would not understand the bad kind of daring
    nor study it. I hate the women who dare so.
    But if somehow with philtres and with magic charms
    practised on Heracles I could defeat this girl,
    why, the deed has been contrived—unless you think
    I am acting wildly. If you do, I am done with it.
CHORUS: If there is any assurance in what is being done you
    seem to us not to have planned badly.
DEIANEIRA: There is this much assurance, that I believe in it,
    but I have not yet put it to the proof.

CHORUS: But you must find out by trial. Even if you think you
    know, you would not know, without trying it.
DEIANEIRA: Well, we shall soon know. I see our messenger here
    at the door, and he will now be on his way.
    Only, cover me with your silence. If you do
    even shameful things in the dark, you are not put to shame.[87]

The passage is a masterpiece of half advice, half assent, half
decision; the Chorus's "but you must find out by trial" is
somewhat falsified in my desperate attempt to translate the
untranslatable. It really means "you have to ('you would
have to') try it before you will ever know." Are they telling
her to go ahead or are they not? Does she say she is going
ahead or does she not? She says it only by implication; but
she chooses also in action, Sophocles' "proof" or "trial," when
Lichas, the courier, appears and she hands him the object.

    With, of course, deadly result. The poisoned blood is the
charm. It eats the flesh of Heracles. That is why and how
he will never love another woman more.

    The tragic choice, then, does not come out hard and
simple. It is complicated by a double deception; deception
of the men, who are not to be told what the gift is or why
it is being sent, because the women feel uneasily that there
is something not quite respectable about the whole business,
at least it is much too private to let the men in on; and
again, self-deception, for if Deianeira had known what the
shirt would do, she never would have sent it; so, in a way,
an extension of the Aristotelian *hamartia,* a mistake of
identities. Yet, with all its indecisions, it is a choice as fatally
necessary as if the fates in person were made to decree it, and
far more convincing. For, once the idea of sending the
shirt, or love charm, has been raised as a possible course of
action, it *has* to go through; neither the curiosity of the

female character with her confidantes, nor of the male spectators, will let it be put away and forgotten, once it has been raised. This is destiny and fate, not theological, but psychological and dramatic.

In *The Women of Trachis,* then, we seem to be able to isolate a moment of choice between two ways, almost, if we cut through the doubts and hesitancies of the character, as boldly shaped as in Herodotus: a moment toward which all preceding action has been developed, from which all subsequent action results. But before we can say that this, dramatic choice, is *the* master pattern which shapes tragedy, we must consider the fact that, while some tragedies have not one choice but a large number, or no major choice but minor choices, others seem to do virtually without choice.

There are minor choices, fully dramatized. In the *Heracles* of Euripides, the hero returns just in time to rescue his wife and children from the murderous clutches of a tyrant called Lycus; but immediately afterwards he is driven mad by Madness, Lyssa, a dramatic character sent against him by Hera; and he murders his family. When he recovers his reason, he contemplates suicide, but decides to live. Morally, the choice of life has more significance than the murder, but it is only a question of what to do with the pieces picked up after the explosion. The explosion itself involved no human choice whatever.[88] In *Andromache,* the heroine is offered a choice between her own life and that of her son.[89] She chooses her son's; but there is no result, both are rescued, and Andromache herself disappears from the last half of her play, which is concerned with the fortunes of Neoptolemus, her husband, whom she does not love, and who never appears on stage at all. In *Iphigeneia in Aulis,* the heroine's choice of self-sacrifice decides the major, sole issue of the play; in *The Heracleidae* and *The Phoenician Women,* similar choices are made by minor characters to authorize minor episodes which yet have their bearing on the total action.[90] But what is major and what is minor? In *Antigone,* the choices of Creon are as indispensable as the heroine's; in fact, the final tragedy, the subject of the final moralization, is his;[91] where do we draw our somewhat arbitrary lines? But, granting minor choices, we still must ask, first, whether some master choice is necessary to tragic action; and again— whether or not this is so—since it is an authentic pattern, what are its necessary shapes in the form of plot.

III

Patterns of Choice, Revenge and Discovery

L ET us return to the statement of Rivier, which we considered before: that the archetype of the tragic situation is found where the hero confronts alternatives and must make a decision, "capitale, souvent mortelle, toujours irrevocable."[1] Is such emphasized choice, whether we call it major or minor, absolutely necessary to Attic tragedy?

In *The Persians* of Aeschylus for example, it is pretty hard to find. After the catastrophe has happened, we hear Xerxes' mother say that bad counselors kept telling her son that Persia must grow, until he finally planned his monstrous expedition.[2] This is a faint afterthought compared with the great sequence in Herodotus where the king, flanked between the bad positive and the good negative counselor, chooses his course, then tries to reverse it, and finds he cannot.[3] In Aeschylus, there is more life and force in what the chorus says: Ate (Infatuation) seduces and pulls; Moira, fate or the way things happen, pushes; so much for choice.[4]

Sophocles' *Electra,* which covers precisely the same stretch of heroic action as *The Libation Bearers* of Aeschylus and *Electra* of Euripides, glaringly lacks the moment of "What shall I do? Can I kill my mother?"—and subsequent agonized choice. For a quite different reason, the moment of choice in *Oedipus Tyrannus* is lacking: here is no question of "What shall I do?," but "Who am I?" and "What have I done?" In *The Trojan Women,* everything has been done to these women; helpless captives have no choice. The only promise of it comes in the question, what shall Menelaus do with Helen? Without a moment's consideration, Hecuba tries to make him kill her. Menelaus makes his decision, a wobbly one; he will take Helen home and kill her there; nobody, on stage or in the audience, is deceived for one moment.[5] In *Iphigeneia in Tauris* we have, in passing, the choice of Orestes to be sacrified rather than accept the offer of Pylades, his friend;[6] this leads, ingeniously, not to death but to recognition; and ultimately, escape. But the heroes do not have to decide *whether* to try to escape; they only decide *how.*

Thus, briefly: we find the pure moment of choice is lacking from the type of play where the events are shaped not toward initiating new action but toward the revelation of the past; call it the discovery play, or the truth-action. It is lacking from (these stories do not exclude each other) the pride-and-punishment story; from the revenge story in its purest form; and from the escape story.[7] For various reasons. Pride-and-punishment, offence against the gods, requires at least the illusion of voluntary action, but impulse rather than choice: we should not expect to find Niobe deciding whether or not to boast of her superiority over Leto. The revenge story insofar as it is purely that, and the escape story, dramatize not the question of what to do, but how to do it. Even Medea, deciding to kill her children, is not deciding that she will punish Jason; she is choosing the most effective way to hurt him. Yet again, here this most effective means will react so cruelly on herself that she does consider discarding her original course of action—a course presumably chosen at first because it seemed self-evident—

of punishing Jason: and the moment is transposed into some-think like the full tragic choice, after all.[8]

Such choice then, as defined by Rivier and considered by us, does constitute an important tragic pattern; but like other patterns, its lines must not be drawn too tight.

The study of Greek poetry is haunted by half-truths, which their authors commonly try to inflate into whole truths. Let me add one, which is perhaps no more than a fancy. Say that, in *The Iliad,* fate is just the plot, the script, the traditional story, the given. The free agent manipulating, with limited authority, this material, is the author, repre-sented by the gods. Particularly, Zeus represents him. Thus at one point Zeus, or the author, is faced with killing a favorite character, Sarpedon; for it is fated, given (in the script), that Sarpedon must die. But the act of authorization is represented as a free choice. Do it if you will, says Hera, that is, save him, but we other gods will not approve: the story violated and wrongly told will bring the disaster of disapproval down on the head of the teller. With tears of blood, Zeus authorizes the death of Sarpedon: his son, in fact; but our explanation is a half-truth, if it is so much as that, a fancy, and we must not press it further. But we can still say that Zeus and Homer alike are faced with a kind of indefinite "it" which makes, at times, their godlike power something which they find it impossible to use.[9]

The tragic poets, with many main lines of their stories fixed, as we have seen, are obsessed with fatality. Yet, where new action is to be initiated, there is an aversion against re-ducing the persons to puppets moved by creatures of over-whelmingly superior force. For such creatures, then, in turn, become persons; this happens in Euripides' *Heracles.* Rather, they prefer to arrange their materials so as to allow for the forcible activity of the human will: or at least the illusion of such activity.

Such an urge to represent choice seems to appear, not only in the numerous minor situations of choice, but in scenes which dramatize a choice that has no actual bearing on the ensuing action, in any sense; and scenes where, it may be argued, there is an illusion of choice where in fact there was no choice at all. Both kinds of scene can be illustrated from *Agamemnon*.

If we view the action in *Agamemnon* as a whole, the master choice is surely that of Clytaemestra: to kill her husband. But Clytaemestra's choosing is never enacted before us. Like the fatal choices of Agamemnon,[10] her choice was made before the action began, and given only in retrospect after the event.[11] What Aeschylus enacts instead is the curious little scene where Agamemnon is persuaded, against his will but by his own free choice, to enter the house, on a carpet of sea-purple, exactly as his wife desires him to.

> Give way to me. Of your own will yield me control.[12]

The choice has no bearing on the event. He will be killed, whatever he does. Yet he is made to make the choice, with many misgivings, like Gyges, as if he were deciding his own destiny.[13]

The crucial choice made by Agamemnon, ten years before, is remembered in our presence by the Chorus near the opening of the play. It came when Agamemnon recognized as a necessity the sacrifice of his daughter, Iphigeneia. Professor Page has shown, as I believe, that *if* we assemble and logically test all the facts and possibilities in the situation, Agamemnon had no choice at all: that is at least, there was no course of action that would save Iphigeneia.[14] But

Aeschylus did not assemble and reasonably so analyze the facts and possibilities; he presented the preparation for the act as a choice—"What shall I do?"—a decision characterized by a heaping of terms of moral disapproval which could not reasonably be applied to an act squeezed out under overwhelming pressure.[15] "When he had assumed the yoke-strap of necessity,"[16] says Aeschylus, his own nature took on the fierceness which would enable him to carry out the act. This means, I think, not that the decision was forced, but its consequence—remembering as I do the quite independent passage in Plato,[17] where the soul chooses a life which will then be controlled by *anangke,* necessity; but the soul is responsible, the god is not; once you have shot the arrow or the bullet, not all your goodwill or pity will stop it. That is *anangke.*

The choice was irrevocable, unless the god intervened.

> What happened next I saw not, neither speak it.
> The crafts of Calchas fail not of outcome.[18]

"The sacrifice itself could not be more impressively told than by this terrible hint" (Sidgwick).[19] Perhaps so; but perhaps here is the final illusion. For as I suppose, both Aeschylus and his audience well understood that the god did intervene, and Iphigeneia was not sacrificed at all but miraculously, and secretly, rescued and transformed. Among early authorities, only Pindar, probably in 474 B.C., said she was slaughtered;[20] her rescue was acknowledged in both the Homeric and the Hesiodic lines of epic, by Sophocles and Euripides, by Polyidos, and probably by Aeschylus himself in his lost *Iphigeneia*;[21] for Aristotle, when he discusses the hypothetical case of a poet, any poet, making a draft for a play using the Iphigeneia-story, simply assumes her rescue as part of the accepted legend.[22] As in some versions of the story of Troy, according to which Helen never fled with Paris at all, so, in this case, the slaughtered Iphigeneia would be a wraith, an illusion, whose fictitious quality did nothing to diminish the deadly effect.

In Professor Rivier's statement, the hero's choice is called "always irrevocable." This is the natural shape of the pattern: at the forking of the ways, when one way is chosen and advance along it has begun, the other way is excluded forever. Individual cases will supply their own reasons to make this clear. Once the very question of sending the poisonous love-charm has been raised by Deianeira, she cannot, as we have seen, drop it, without becoming dramatically incredible.[23] Once Medea has stated that she will murder her children, she cannot, dramatically, change her mind; a real-life woman, of course, could do so and probably would; but then her action would have faded into that limbo of actual or plausible events that do not make a story. Her hesitations and reversals have the effect of making her realistic, but only emphasize the irrevocability of her choice once it has been made.[24] When Eteocles has chosen, the language shows him as swept on in a momentum (*anangke*) now beyond his control.[25] Though it was hardly a matter of choice to begin with, Oedipus also finds himself carried on by momentum to learn the hateful truth the moment before he learns it.

> HERDSMAN: Oh, I am at the very point of dreadful speaking.
> OEDIPUS: And I of dreadful hearing. But it must be heard.[26]

The impersonal form expresses the pattern at work.

And yet, there are definite cases in tragedy when, once

the choice, which should be fatal, has been made, its effects
are nevertheless canceled: and even when a decisive choice,
once made, is then effectively unmade.

It can be done by divine fiat, the god from the machine.
In *Iphigeneia in Aulis,* Agamemnon tries to undo his decision
to sacrifice Iphigeneia. He is thwarted by Menelaus, who
insists. But Menelaus then repents and tries to change his
own decision. It is too late. Iphigeneia seems to save all the
rules of action by volunteering to die, as an act of free choice.
But Artemis saves her, thereby rendering effective the once-
futile efforts of the principals to revoke their decisions and
turn back the progress of *anangke* which had issued from
their choices.[27]

Again, in plays of misidentification, dramatic choice may
be automatically revoked as soon as the true identification
is made. This might be illustrated from *Ion.* Ion is Creusa's
lost, unrecognized son. Creusa has tried to poison him,
thinking him to be her husband's bastard. She has been
caught, sentenced to death by the Delphians, and Ion is
about to drag her from the altar for execution, when the
recognition scene occurs. The mutually murderous intentions vanish at once.[28] But the choices, in this play, have
never been emphasized; if it is permissible to push my typical
terms so far, I will say that this melodrama, combining the
foundling story with the revenge play, never gave scope for
a full dramatic choice.

Very rarely, a decision is revoked through persuasion. In
Ajax, Agamemnon seems resolved to refuse the dead hero
his due burial; Odysseus persuades him to permit it. But
Agamemnon is merely a hostile judge, not a full dramatic
character who commands interest for his own sake, and his
decision moreover is assumed from his general attitude,

never dramatized as a difficult, agonizing choice.[29] In *Heraclēs*, the hero who has killed wife and children in a fit of madness, assumes, rather than decides, that he must kill himself; Theseus persuades him that it is braver and stronger to dree his weird and live.[30] In such cases, a moral point has been established by sound rhetoric, but we lack that effect of dramatic compulsion which comes from the concerted drive of character and circumstance.

There remains the *Philoctetes* of Sophocles. The Legend of Philoctetes is as follows. He had been Heracles' friend, and was heir and master of the bow of Heracles. He joined the expedition against Troy. On the way, he was bitten by a snake. The wound did not kill him, but festered, stank, and made him cry out with pain. The Achaeans marooned him on a desolate island where he languished for nearly ten years; but at last they realized that they needed him and his bow in order to capture Troy. An embassy was sent to bring him back. Philoctetes did return to Troy, was healed of his wound, killed Paris, and played a major part in the final victory.

Such are the compulsory elements of the Legend, which itself follows the pattern story of the necessary man.[31] The story of Philoctetes was used for at least eight Athenian tragedies, including two by Sophocles and one each by Aeschylus and Euripides. Only *Philoctetes* (*on Lemnos*) by Sophocles has survived.[32]

The bare outline of the Legend forces a change on the part of Philoctetes. He must be unwilling to return; else there is no subject for a tragedy. The unwillingness must be overcome (despite the presence of those who have injured him); else the conclusion dictated by the Legend is not secured. How to do this is the dramatist's problem, and the

Legend leaves him free. By force, that is, trickery, deception, and stealing his bow? By persuasion? Euripides brought in a rival embassy from Troy.[33] By the intervention of divinity? Or by a combination of means?

Sophocles made his hero fight down persuasion and treacherous force alike, only to yield to the god from the machine, the deified Heracles, his old friend; a sort of combination of divine fiat (since the schedule he proposes comes from Zeus) and persuasion (since Heracles speaks as an urgent friend, not a superior).

But the choice of Philoctetes is not the only tragic choice in this play. Sophocles makes Odysseus arrive on his errand accompanied by Neoptolemus, the young, strong son of dead Achilles. The strategy of Odysseus must be carried out by the new man, for Odysseus is known and hated; Neoptolemus must pretend to have his own quarrel with the Achaeans, and so win the sympathy of Philoctetes and ultimately his bow and his person. The young warrior objects, for he and Odysseus both know that straight force, not guile and deception, is his natural way of dealing; but he yields to the older man's reasoning, and accepts his task.

> So be it. I will put away all shame. I will do it.[34]

The subsequent action records the undoing of that choice, by painful stages. Neoptolemus finds he cannot continue the deception, and tells Philoctetes the whole story; he has been entrusted with the bow; he returns it; he is still trying to persuade the man to come to Troy of his own free will; it is useless; and at last he is willing to take Philoctetes home, break his promise to Odysseus, lose all his future for the sake of this too stubborn man and for the sake of being true to his own nature. The Trojan expedition, the fate of

the world, the Legend, are on the point of defeat, the whole
cause lost, when the Legend is rescued by the Supernatural.
Or is it the Supernatural? Nothing in the lines forbids us to
think that this *deux ex machina* is a contrivance, the last
stratagem of Odysseus, which none the less coincides with
the true will of Heracles and Zeus.[35]

Be that as it may, Sophocles has sacrificed something to
secure, not the rescue of the Legend—this could have been,
and actually was, otherwise done, in other tragedies—but
its fulfilment in concord with the truth-to-nature of its
characters, and the moral which is the key to the play,
stated in this one case with complete simplicity.

> All becomes hard when a man, leaving his own nature,
> tries to act in a way that is not his.[36]

The first choice of Neoptolemus was false. He said he
would put away all shame. He could not do it. The true
choice, the answer to the question.

> O Zeus, what shall I do?[37]

is to revoke his old false choice and break his promise to
Odysseus.

Philoctetes is unique among the Attic tragedies that have
come down to us, seeming somehow most modern in the
prevalence of sheer character over *anangke* or pattern. The
more classical way is that of *Antigone*. Her choice, and that
of Creon, once made, will permit no deviation. Creon tries.
It is too late, useless. Antigone herself at the end sees that
she may have failed, falls back on desperate reasoning to
justify her choices,[38] but will not, cannot, change. A last-
minute recantation or rescue, perfectly plausible in real life,
would make the whole drama meaningless.

Choice: The Suppliant Play

The pattern of choice, so far considered, is exceedingly simple in itself, yet in its simplest form can grow into a complication of choice and action, as we, perhaps, have seen. There are, in addition, at least two special choice-patterns to be considered. One is the suppliant story (or the king's choice), told in *The Suppliant Maidens* of Aeschylus, *The Heracleidae* and *The Suppliant Women* of Euripides, *Oedipus at Colonus* by Sophocles, and presumably the lost *Heracleidae* of Aeschylus.[39] Athenian historical tradition, according to Thucydides,[40] made Athens in the heroic age a place of refuge for unfortunate nobles who had been driven by war or dynastic quarrels out of their own possessions. In the suppliant play, a group helpless and perse-cuted, takes refuge at Athens (Argos in *The Suppliant Maidens* of Aeschylus). If the king accepts them, he will bring war on his state: if he refuses, he risks the disapproval of gods and men for spurning the religious usages of the Greeks. He must choose, under pressure of his own con-science, plus the external pressures: the appeal of the sup-pliants, who may have an advocate to plead for them: the threats of the persecuting power, mostly represented by a herald. He chooses to protect the suppliants. A battle follows, reported by messenger; in every case but one the righteous cause triumphs.[41]

This is plainly a compulsive pattern, but the story was not very frequently used. It is hard to make a complete tragedy out of it. *The Suppliant Maidens* of Aeschylus is the first act of a connected trilogy and is mainly choral. Euripides pieces his suppliant-dramas out, adding in one case a virgin-sacrifice and a revenge-story, in the other a *laudatio* of the dead and *Liebestod*.[42] The pattern tends to produce a debate on public issues (democracy against autocracy, international religion and humanity against nationalistic politics, virtue against expediency) rather than a dramatic action; a situation both public and stock tends to produce stock characters: the king, the herald. Yet certain original effects are secured by Aeschylus and Sophocles when, using the structure of the pattern, they succeed in adding a new dimension. In *The Eumenides*, the refugee group becomes the virtuous murderer, Orestes: the persecuting power, the Eumenides: the king who chooses, Athene combining with the Athenian jurymen: and the persons ultimately concerned, the whole world of gods and men. Sophocles plainly had little interest in the public suppliant play, of which his fragments indicate no cases. The Euripidean type does not give much room for choice and character. In *Oedipus at Colonus,* Sophocles' king, Theseus, is an autocrat who decides what hardly seems to be a public question by private decree, his herald is Creon himself, his Oedipus does not plead, and celebrates his own attainment of mercy by rejecting and cursing his son, Polyneices, who has come as a suppliant to him.

Choice: The Sacrifice Play

One more pattern involving choice is seen in the story of human sacrifice. What might be called the standard situation, with its solution, is as follows. The welfare of the State, or the success of some great enterprise, has been threatened; there will be general disaster, unless a divinity is appeased. The divinity demands a human sacrifice, generally a virgin princess.[43] For the one candidate who will precisely satisfy the conditions, substitutes may be suggested, and rejected. The victim declares herself willing to die, and the sacrifice becomes not so much a sacrifice with the human being substituted for the ordinary animal, as an act of self-devotion.

In *Iphigeneia in Aulis,* as we have seen, this action supports the entire play, in which the climax comes when the heroine chooses death of her own free will. Sacrifice was also probably the main story of Euripides' lost *Erechtheus.* Here, whether or not the fated daughter chose her death,[44] dramatic point was made of the moment when Praxithea, the girl's mother, decided (unlike the other parents in such situations) that she was willing to have her daughter die for the State's good; for we possess a sizeable fragment containing the celebrated, and intolerably smug, speech of the queen announcing the decision, which somehow loses all its human pathos when the accepted death has to be died by somebody else and not the speaker.[45] The voluntary sacrifice makes an important minor incident in *The Heracleidae* and *The Phoenician Women* of Euripides, constitutes the first half of Euripides' *Hecuba,* and may have been an important part of the lost *Andromedas* by Sophocles and Euripides.[46] Sophocles also wrote a *Polyxena,* but we do not know the details of the choice.[47]

The story of the public sacrifice of a virgin, as we have outlined it, is one particular mode for pre-setting a necessary, fated action into which the principal gears herself so that it becomes not merely an act of bloody brutality inflicted by overwhelming force, but a choice of honor.[48] By shifting an element here and there, altering a dimension or an emphasis, quite other effects are obtained. A special highlight on Iphigeneia and Polyxena is their physical beauty, the allure of sex.[49] It is not just that no ugly duckling is fit for sacrifice. Their lyric dimension is as the bride of death, the echo of the *fabula sacra* of Persephone.[50] It relates them to Antigone, who chose death in so different a setting.[51] Quite at the other end of the scale, but still contiguous to the whole larger pattern, is the self-immolation of the hero: who does not, however, submit to sacrifice but goes down fighting where he knows he must be killed, for the gods are said to demand his life as the price of victory for his side. In actual history this may be after all why Leonidas died at Thermopylae.[52] In drama it seems to lurk beneath Eteocles' choice in *The Seven,* and was probably prominent in the plays, by Sophocles and Euripides, which dealt with Protesilaus: the first man to land from the ships at Troy must be killed in combat, and the first man off was, by his own choice, Protesilaus.[53]

By shifting, again, one more element, we find new kinds of situation and character. Suppose this self-immolation is not public, but private, for the sake of no Trojan War or Helen, but the hero himself, or his family: then we have Ajax and Antigone, and Alcestis. The last refinement is the *Liebestod,* the unwillingness to survive the death of the beloved one; Euadne leaps from a height to join the body of Capaneus in Euripides' *Suppliant Women,* Laodameia dies on a pyre for her lost Protesilaus in his play named after that hero.[54] The story seems, not surprisingly, to be peculiar to Euripides; but Aeschylus may have exploited it, on a hint from Homer, in his lost Achilles-trilogy, making Achilles as Patroclus's lover unwilling to survive him.[55]

Yet all these transpositions into such different plots have this in common, that they do pre-set a pattern in which death, whether or not by divine orders, is seen to be necessary, and in which the hero sees this, consents, and makes the act his own.

The Revenge Play

The same actions, however, taken not as the central story which is acted out, but as background outside the play for a given situation which now exists, may produce an entirely different kind of play which is no longer the tragedy of choice. The sacrifice of Iphigeneia—saved but believed dead —serves as original motive for the mightiest revenge-series in tragedy.

> Was it Iphigeneia, who at the Euripus crossing
> was slaughtered far from home,
> that vexed her to drive in anger the hand of violence?[56]

The revenge pattern in its purest form assumes or merely states the why, the causes, and asks not what to do, but how. The classic revenge play is the *Electra* of Sophocles. We might take as the key Apollo's sanction reported by Orestes at the very outset:

> Phoebus answered me thus, and you shall hear it now.
> Without an army or force of arms my hand must work
> this just slaughter by deception and treachery.[57]

So the question of whether to kill his mother is noted in transit, granted, as attributive adjective: the positive counsel generates the liar's tragedy, the false messenger, the monologue over the empty urn; and—with the return of justice— the bleak moral at the end:

> There should be such prompt justice for all of those
> who try to act beyond what law allows.
> Kill them. And there would not be much villainy left.[58]

Since a mere crushing of the unrighteous by force of arms gives no suspense, complication, or scope for story-telling, the treachery is dramatically essential, and the corpus of lost tragedy is full of stories of revenge on usurpers whose guilt offers (apparently) no problems of morals, but whose strength of position poses elaborate problems of means for the avengers.

For the Electra-story, Sophocles alone of the three sur-viving tragedians was content to see the action ended and all problems solved in the execution of criminals. Aeschylus, using both the full scale of the trilogy and his long prophetic lyrics which look behind and ahead of the development in present action, absorbed the particular revenge-action into a whole series, where crime generates vindictive counter-crime, until the end is reached in voluntary renunciation of vengeance.

> The children were eaten: there was the first
> affliction, the curse of Thyestes.
> Next came the royal death, when a man
> and lord of Achaean armies went down
> killed in the bath. Third
> is for the savior. He came. Shall I call
> it that, or death? Where
> is the end? Where shall the fury of fate
> be stilled to sleep, be done with?[59]

Thus ends *The Libation Bearers*. The whole trilogy ends with Orestes cleared, the Furies of the mother appeased. Eurip-ides does not so reconcile his elements. What he does has been well expressed by Professor Dodds: "In his revenge plays—*Medea, Hecuba, Electra*—the spectator's sympathy is first enlisted for the avenger and then made to extend to the avenger's victims. *The Bacchae* is constructed on the same principle."[60] To this list I would add, from the extant plays, *The Heracleidae*. This may be called a moral pattern, but

anything which so involves the subjective factor as "enlist-
ment of sympathy" is not exactly a story-pattern in the
sense in which I have been using the term. This, in the
revenge play, directs the kind of means by which revenge
is exacted. Recovery of lost vengeance-plays would tell us
more. When the villain was hoist by his own petard; when
Polydectes was turned to stone by the gorgon's head he had
sent Perseus to win;[61] when Dirce was ploughed under by
the oxen with whom she planned to destroy Antiope;[62] was
sympathy for the final victim directed, or were these
villains indeed, whose death was simple poetic justice
through their own wicked designs?

The Pattern of the Lost One

Iphigeneia's supposed slaughter becomes, in retrospect, not
the drama of the sacrificed virgin but a motive for the
revenge play. But Iphigeneia was rescued: thought to be
dead, in truth miraculously carried away to a remote place.[63]
If we resume her story there, the sacrifice-scene recedes into
the background of pre-dramatic motive and cause. She is
now the lost loved one, awaiting reunion, identification (by
tokens),[64] rescue, and restoration. That is now her story and
her fate. It has often been noticed that the plots of *Iphigeneia
in Tauris* and *Helen* are closely analogous.[65] Helen too was
saved when Hermes snatched her away from home and set
her down in Egypt, at the end of the world, there to await
identification and recovery. Meanwhile, the false image
which represented her false immorality worked havoc in the
world, as the false sacrifice of Iphigeneia had done. As
Orestes, a brother, to Iphigeneia, so the long-lost husband
rescued came to Helen. The Greeks outwitted the Bar-
barians to escape them, but the final escape was sanctioned

by the god from the machine, who pacified everybody and tied up all the details of the story once for all. The parallel between Helen and the sacrificial virgin extends even to details. Helen, the housewife and mother, enacts death and the maiden; like Persephone, she was snatched away while gathering flowers in the meadow;[66] and the lyric chorus sings the *fabula sacra* of Demeter's desolation and anger over the loss of her daughter.[67]

The theme of *Helen,* beyond all other extant Greek plays, is illusion. All dramas which are truth-plays: the foundling stories; the stories of lost persons recovered, of mistaken identity; the stories of character defamed and vindicated; all have this in common. A lie has been perpetrated on the dramatic world. However lively the activity, it is all shaped toward the revelation of the truth: which comes, indeed, after the darkest moment. As, in the dramas of choice and action, the debacle comes just after an outburst of false joy and hope:[68] so in the truth patterns the truth is rescued after the lie seems sure to prevail—the oracles of Oedipus discredited, Menelaus rejecting the true Helen and clinging to the false dream.[69]

The Indestructible Man

Dramas of choice and dramas of discovery—new action, old truth—are the two extremes of the story-types which generate the patterns which we have considered. Yet they can be combined. In addition to the revenge-play, there is another form of pattern which in itself seems to combine the two. This might be called the destruction of the indestructible man.

The Legend offers the following material.

Meleager was killed by his mother: with curses, and/or

by means of the firebrand which, when burnt up, would end his life: because he killed her brother(s) for the sake of a woman.[70]

Heracles was killed by his wife and, at the end, by his own act; for jealousy over his faithlessness, through the poisoned shirt of the dead Nessus.[71]

Ajax was killed by himself: with the sword of the dead Hector: in his one fatal spot.[72]

Odysseus was killed by his son Telegonus, whom Circe bore him: with the tail of a sting ray,[73] the only weapon which could kill him.

I give, not the plots of individual plays, but selected details in the compendious mass of legend which was available to the tragic poets and from which they could as usual select or reject at discretion. We do not have a strict pattern here, apparently; and the loss of crucial plays has obscured the lines. But there are certain features in common. Each of these heroes is the greatest man of his time, or at least his time and place. Heracles' greatness is unquestioned. Meleager is compared only with Achilles and Heracles, who are given as later than he.[74] Ajax after the death of Achilles is generally regarded as the greatest man at Troy.[75] Odysseus at Troy is barely of the first magnitude as a warrior; Odysseus in ogreland is overmatched and must use wits, not force; but Odysseus in the western world of the suitors is supreme beyond challenge.[76]

To have the invincible man go on to meet one who is stronger yet: to have Heracles meet one monster too many and too big: this is simply not proper story-telling. Then the invincible man is not invincible; this is what happens to Hector;[77] *impar congressus Achilli* is a story, but not this one.[78] How then shall he be destroyed? Because there is no dramatic point to having an indestructible man unless you are going to destroy him. There is the hint of magic, the fatal gift, the "no living man" (but a dead one!), the fatal weapon and/or the one fatal spot in the otherwise impervious hero. But we have the moral cause as well: the hero falls not to some great enemy but to a friend, in the Greek sense, a *philos,* a near and dear one, or himself. Through offense, some injury he has done; we are almost with the old ghost of *hamartia.* Ultimately or directly he is destroyed by himself,[79] and it is a truth action after all—most dramatically stated when Heracles in *The Women of Trachis* sees the pattern of his life and its meaning—the solution of the puzzle.[80] The invulnerable man was not invulnerable: the truth is out, the lie dispelled. "Even Heracles died" is a consolation.[81] All men are mortal. And the hero is a man. And the greatest hero is not greater than the sum of himself.

IV

Character, Imagery, Rhetoric, Ceremony

ET no one think that I think that in these past analyses
I have exhausted the meaning of tragedy or explained
its structure. I have not even exhausted the evident
story-patterns; whoever cares to look through the texts for
more, will find them. Also, the scrutiny of formal elements
is bound to leave the scrutinizer with a one-sided or partial
view.

I have tried to isolate some cases where it is clear that the
story, both as given and as created, has certain rights of its
own. The aspect of tragedy in which these rights are
especially felt is its dramatic aspect, as telling a story through
miming it or acting it out. There are many other aspects
which make tragedy what it is, and in these aspects too there
are compulsions, rights, designs. Tragedies are not only
narrative and dramatic, but lyrical, ceremonial, ethical or
projective of character, rhetorical, and religious. I would
conclude by attempting to do some justice to some of these
aspects, in connection always with the narrative-dramatic
substrate.

In his lyric drama, Aeschylus complicates a whole network
of imagery. In *The Oresteia,* there is the she-viper who
mates and kills her husband; the young vipers who kill their
mother; the poison of the snake working inside; so, secret
sickness long buried, waiting to break out; grief of memory;
the escape and pursuit of dreams; the amorous mishandling;

wrong done and rankling; so, the overthrowing of idols, the wrecking of ideals; fault in the house, leak in the ship or bewilderment of its helmsman. These situations of image are projected in the given story out of Legend, the "play" as such, where plot is minimal. In the most choral of Aeschylus's plays, *The Suppliant Maidens,* the action seems to be simply a miming out of the dominant image-scheme: flight; pursuit; refuge: the helpless animal, calf or dove; the ravening pursuer, wolf, hawk; the strong protector.

In Sophocles, the lyric suggests rather than states. It makes a cloud around the sharp, clear choice of Antigone; imagining the bride of Hades, nubile, not defiant; the refused story of star-crossed lovers; the buried beauty; the cutting-off of the last loveliest shoot of the great tree of the house of Oedipus. In *Oedipus,* it conjures up the wanderer from and in the mountain wilderness, the lost illusive murderer, wild man or wild bull, hunted, pushed off by those who are trying to find him or help him—all pinned into the pattern-story of the foundling. But the action before the eye, characters choosing or deceiving, must always dominate the Sophoclean drama as we have it. In *Philoctetes* the lyric element is almost gone, surviving mostly in the pathos of things: the bow itself; the cave, the pitiful little one-man settlement; the spirits of the lonely rock.

Euripides tends to tie his complicated actions together by repeated words or thematic ideas. Sometimes there seem to be key words, not, I think, chosen as such and planted, but terms that haunt him through the writing of an action (habits grew on Euripides). In *Hippolytus* we have *nosos* (sickness) for Phaedra, *semnos* (superior) for Hippolytus; in *The Heracleidae, eleutheria* (liberty); in *Heracles, kallinikos* (glorious victor) to celebrate the simple triumphant strength

of the hero in its mockery and ruin; in *The Trojan Women,*
pyrgoi (fortified walls). Elsewhere, more in the manner of
Aeschylus but hovering over plots far more advanced and
intricate, we have word groups expressive of ideas: in *Helen,*
appearance and reality (or truth) where the thing seen clear
but false has sickened the world; in *The Bacchae* the mountain, with its forests; and on the mountain, the hunt, of beasts
or men.

The people of tragedy, with their personalities, are, of
course, mainly the population of Legend, which was available to the fifth-century poets; plus various minor characters invented or filled out at will. The structure of tragedy
itself dictates certain persons who are scarcely characters at
all, but mere announcers for the author: the ordinary messenger is a good case, and there is always the chorus. On the
other hand, certain familiar heroes and heroines, such as
Achilles, Odysseus, Theseus, Heracles, had by the fifth
century a status practically as historical persons; sometimes,
as in the case of the Homeric heroes, their characters were
fixed long before tragic poetry began.[1] The question is, how
far did their stories permit the tragic poets to develop
character as such, and how far did they do so? Answers here
must necessarily be partly subjective.

Stories to some extent dictate characters to act them. Let
us take an early case. Suppose, what may very well be true,
that Homer invented the episode of Polyphemus. The hero
in such an adventure must be Odysseus; at least, it is un-
thinkable that it should be Achilles, for the story requires a
monster far beyond the human scale of size and strength, and
to confront Achilles with such would be downright em-
barrassing. Like father like son. You can scarcely imagine
Neoptolemus in the story of Telemachus among the suitors.

This calls for a young man who always thinks before he acts. If he sees he cannot act, he waits. A Neoptolemus must have assailed the suitors headlong and gone down over-whelmed by superior numbers. It would hardly have made a story.[2]

Yet if the persons of the heroic world are fixed, they are fluid as well, and their stories, in variants, can vary them. Consider, once more, Helen in Euripides. In *Helen* she is the long-lost wife waiting to be reclaimed by her wandering husband. Then, she *must* be the patient, virtuous beauty. Once grant the great illusion that keys this play, there she is, all comes clear. It does not mean that Euripides has recanted, disowned his usual concept of Helen. The steely glamor-girl of *The Trojan Women* will be back again in *Orestes,* absorbed in keeping her maturing charms immaculate and patronizing a dishevelled Electra. In *Iphigeneia in Tauris,* Orestes is the wandering prince who finds his long-lost sister. The furies of his murdered mother, whether in the form of outward monsters or mental sickness, have necessarily shrunk. He has occasional fits; otherwise he is the strong good young man who suits the story of recognition and escape, an optimistic kind of play by a poet who was no confirmed optimist. The past is the occasion for wandering, otherwise there is little time for it. The pattern compels. But the sick young man will be back in *Orestes.*

The more the situation or pattern is a stock situation or pattern, the more, it seems, it creates standard characters. So it is in Aristophanic comedy which, beneath its wild dis-orders, preserves a traditional form more strict than tragedy demands. The preposterous scheme of the comic hero, too quaintly reasonable for real life, succeeds gloriously, and breeds a procession of greedy phony gate-crashers who try to crowd in on blessings they have done nothing to deserve. They are much alike in character and they answer the situation.

To return, however, to tragedy: the truth actions and revenge actions with their emphasis on the logic of the plot show, broadly speaking, less interest in the special, private natures of the persons involved. On the other hand, choice is character; and the minimum of personality is that which will make the choice made seem necessary and inevitable. Or better, perhaps, whether or not the drama is mainly of choice, the hero must be sufficient to the action, whatever it is.

Sometimes, indeed, this sufficiency is not fully shown in the character's own actions, but must be taken for granted, or even shored up by external statements. *The Women of Trachis* shows, as we have seen, the destruction of Heracles, the indestructible man, through those secret entrances that such a man's nature and history allow. This Heracles is called by the persons of the play in all sincerity "the greatest of men."[3] That is what he ought to be. In the story as told here, he has used his great strength not to destroy malignant monsters and help mankind, but to destroy and ravish a Greek city in cruel vengeance for an injury he had deserved; he showed not only brutality but cowardice, *hybris* or foul play, pushing a friend from a tower when he was looking the other way.[4] But the greatness and good achievements of Heracles are "given"; they are what "everybody knows"; and the person comes out barely sufficient and credible as the hero who commanded the love of Deianeira and the devotion of Hyllus, who recognizes and directs his own finishing, which is catastrophe for the world. In *Oedipus,* the great intelligence of the hero is requisite. In the action, that intelligence jumps to wrong conclusions again and again.[5] Its only success you can name is the defeat of the Sphinx. Yet the opening scene, the way in which his people turn to Oedipus in their trouble, sufficiently establishes him as one who has ruled wisely and well, with unbroken success; until now.

Sometimes again the projected tragedy requires careful selection from the attributes provided by the Legend for a given heroic character. When Sophocles told the story of the self-immolation of Ajax, he could not take over the full-drawn character of *The Iliad:* the sturdiest, steadiest, least temperamental, and most modest of the Achaean heroes.[6] He used only the facts of his prowess, his particular rivalry with Hector, and his independence of divine aid.[7] In *The Women of Trachis,* the agent of Heracles' destruction is Deianeira:

> no spearman of the plains, no earth born
> army of Giants, no wild animal in his force,
> not Hellas, no barbarian, not all the world
> I traveled through and cleared, none of them
>   could have done it
> but a woman, a female figure, nothing like a man, .
> she alone brought me down, and never touched
>   a sword.[8]

The name Deianeira, "destroyer of a man (or husband)," thus finds its special irony. With that name at some time went the figure of an Amazonian heroine, fit sister of Meleager. In one story, on her travels with Heracles, she put on armor and fought beside her husband and was wounded, all to secure milk for their baby, Hyllus.[9] If Sophocles knew of such stories, he ignored or rejected them. Such a heroine will not fit his pattern, where the world of masculine brutality crashes into the privacy of the sheltered female life, like a bull in the boudoir. And his Deianeira is as female as he can make her, a gentle soul full of feminine fear.[10] The irony is so much the stronger.

In a similar way, Euripides, using Admetus, ignored (if he knew them) the traditions which made him participate in the quest of the Golden Fleece and the Calydonian boar hunt.[11] His story demands, not an adventurous hero, but one of whom the Chorus can say:

> Your luck had been
> good, so you were inexperienced when
> grief came.[12]

Whatever else Euripides may mean by his portrait of Admetus, he is surely represented as one who has hitherto done and suffered little; thus, no Argonaut.

The character is to be sufficient to his choice, or the pattern of his story. As Aristotle said: "They do not act so as to represent character; but through their actions, they take on character."[13] Sufficient. Is that all? Is there to be no personality, no character, for its own sake?

The economy of Greek drama, and of all drama, is a masterful thing. It does not permit what the novel does, a full world, still abstracted, and idealized compared with the world of reality, but well peopled with persons who have dimension and depth. It does not permit Mr. Micawber, George Forsyte, Baron de Charlus, who, whether or not they are active participants in a story with a beginning, middle and end, simply go on being themselves. All readers know the feeling of indignation when a favorite novel is converted into a play or a motion picture, when the major figures are lopped and foreshortened beyond recognition and three or four minor characters are fused into one, or thrown out altogether. The novel simply has more time and place for people, things, backgrounds, than the strict economy of the mimed and spoken story which is drama.[14]

Yet there do remain the big characters, the star parts. The modern actor, playing Hamlet, will not be content with a character-in-action who is just sufficient to play his necessary part in the revenge-drama. He feels he must *be* Hamlet. This is a man, and the play itself has interest chiefly as it concerns him. Are the big characters of Attic tragedy to be so conceived? Did the actors so take them? In truth, as for the actors, the circumstances in which the Athenian trilogies were given are somewhat against this. Hecuba in *The Trojan Women* is an exacting exhausting part. She is on stage from beginning to end. The modern actress who plays her will live herself into being Hecuba. The Athenian male protagonist had presumably to play first Paris (Alexander), then Palamedes, then Hecuba, all on the same morning, one right after another.[15] What was expected of the actor must, to some extent, have influenced the dramatist when he was composing the part.[16]

Beyond this, we cannot go far. To me, those characters are most like independent persons, to be so studied and played, who show some touch of the irrational, some privacies of personality that escape the logic of the plot, are not necessary to it. Hamlet is Hamlet partly because of his hesitations and questionings. So those Attic characters are most personal who chop and change in their choices, or threaten to: Medea inciting herself, Philoctetes and Neoptolemus, Ismene trying to reverse herself. Antigone is in a way most Antigone when at the end, without disowning her choice, she wavers and doubts her conviction that she is serenely right and everyone else is wrong. This is what I feel; somewhere here is the point where each actor, spectator, or reader must begin to fill in and deepen the outlines of the dramatic people from his own experience and imagination.

The actions of tragedy develop not only persons and personalities but also call for the consideration of issues and causes. Characters in conflict, defense, attack, self-examination may express their own individual nature. They may also generalize their problems, classifying them as particular instances under general rules of argument. Here enters the rhetorical element. Rhetoric is a large term; I am content not to go much beyond the minimal definition of *The Shorter Oxford English Dictionary*: "The art of using language so as to persuade or influence others." Even this covers a great deal: not only the attempts by characters to persuade other characters, but the attempts by poets to persuade their audiences: thus, sometimes, Aristotle's *dianoia,* the purpose and point of the action, or parts of it.[17]

Dramatic persons want their way. You cannot always get your way by merely insisting on it, or by using main force. You must often have to persuade by reasoning, or by reason's persuasive counterfeit.

The Suppliant Maidens, the most elemental of tragedies, almost lacks rhetoric as persuasion. The maidens blackmail; the pursuing Egyptians grab. They do not resemble, but are, predatory animals after victims; though even Hesiod's hawk stated his case to the nightingale in his claws.[18] In *The Oresteia,* on the other hand, we have Peitho, Persuasion, at her extremes. In *Agamemnon* the Chorus sees her as the forcible seducing siren.

> Persuasion the persistent overwhelms him,
> she, strong daughter of designing Ruin.[19]

By the end of *The Eumenides* she has grown respectable in
Athene's majestic pleading with the Furies.

> But if you hold Persuasion has her sacred place
> of worship, in the sweet beguilement of my voice,
> then you might wish to stay with us.

>   I admire the eyes
> of Persuasion, who guided the speech of my mouth
> toward these, when they were reluctant and wild.
> Zeus, who guides men's speech in councils, was too
>   strong; and my ambition
> for good wins out in the whole issue.[20]

Indeed, Peitho is everywhere in drama. One character
appeals to another: Tecmessa to Ajax, Neoptolemus to
Philoctetes, the servant to Hippolytus, Teiresias to Pentheus,
countless others to others; mostly, in vain; part of dramatic
action seems to consist in the shaking off of appeals. But
Peitho is also there when the character, without appealing
to anyone, states his position, or any position; whether it be
Prometheus flinging his defiance at Zeus,[21] or Medea
expounding the place of the housewife in the scheme of
things.[22]

A characteristic use of rhetoric in Attic tragedy is seen in
those rather formal debates between persons, where each
states his case in a long *rhesis* or oration, with arguments and
reasons, the set speeches being often followed by a rapid
back-and-forth exchange and punctuated by staid appre-
ciations from the leader of the Chorus.

Such a scene has sometimes been called *The Agon* of the
play, as if it were a regular traditional part of the original
form of tragedy.[23] But *agon* does not seem to be, like

prologue or *parodos* or *stasimon,* an ancient technical term. Moreover, the earliest cases of these formal debates seem to be those between Menelaus and Teucer, then Agamemnon and Teucer, in *Ajax*; Antigone and Creon, Creon and Haemon, in *Antigone*; and Admetus and Pheres in *Alcestis*.[24] It rather seems to be a special Sophoclean form to express the fact of dramatic opposition, which had been expressed in other ways by Aeschylus.

But though we should avoid preconceptions about *The Agon*, it is convenient to call such a scene *an agon,* that is, a *contest.* The resemblance also to a case at law is obvious and has been often noted. In such a case there is no dramatic or, to speak humbly, entertainment value unless there is enough power on both sides to make a match of it. So Menelaus, Creon, Pheres, and other bad or misguided persons are made to give good reasons, or at least to argue eloquently. Here, for instance, is Creon haranguing his son.

> The man who acts with honor in his own household
> will in his city be a worthy citizen.
> I would be always confident that such a man
> will serve well as an officer and soldier too,
> and in the storm of spears that he will stand steadfast
> and fight where he is stationed in the battle line,
> a brave dutiful comrade-in-arms.[25]

These are at least superficially worthy sentiments spoken for a detestable cause. I believe that Creon is wrong all through and we are meant to know it.

As Plato tells us,[26] both Socrates and Gorgias, the master and champion of rhetoric, recognized the power of persuasive eloquence as a dangerous thing. It enables one to "make the worse appear the better case": the charge which killed Socrates.[27] The feeling of distrust was and is akin to what we may feel about the criminal lawyer who secures acquittal or lenience for the ghastliest criminals. The tragic poets noted this themselves. In *The Trojan Women,* after Helen's clever defense Euripides makes his Chorus say:

> Destroy this woman's eloquence. For she speaks well
> and is wicked. That is shocking.[28]

In addition to moral distrust, too much eloquence in tragedy may cause a kind of dramatic distrust as well. For one thing, it stops the action. But it also seems to show too direct an interference by the author in the personal expression of his own creation; or, as Miss Dale has put it: ". . . sometimes the skill of the pleading obscures the woman Alcestis, as when she emphasizes her own virtue in contrast to the conduct of the parents, or when at the end of the speech she says: 'and you, my husband, can boast that you had the noblest of women to wife, and you, my children, that you were born of the noblest of mothers.' It is a pleader's peroration, not the spontaneous cry of a noble heart."[29] So too Creon in *Oedipus Tyrannus,* Hippolytus in his tragedy, both innocent men unjustly accused, seem to spoil their cases by arguing thinly from probabilities.[30] They convince nobody, on stage or off.

Rhetoric, in short, is counter-dramatic when it is superfluous. This is not always the case. In *Medea,* for instance, Jason's long, clever, and condemned[31] speech both expounds rhetorically his side of the argument, and simultaneously, displays that shabby personality which is essential to the plot as we have it. Quite another sort of thing is Antigone's speech to Creon, beginning:

> It was not Zeus who made this proclamation to me,
> nor Justice, she who sits beside the gods below.

> They did not pass your laws.
> Nor did I think that you, a mortal man, had power
> to issue proclamations that would override
> the unwritten and unshaken statutes of the gods.
> These are not of today and yesterday. They live
> forever. No man knows the day when they came forth.[32]

This is rhetoric. It is also blazing drama. And it serves at least four ends essential to this action: to state Antigone's cause, to show her character in support of it, to necessitate subsequent action, since she carries the attack to Creon and forces his hand, and to show one main issue of the tragedy called *Antigone*.

Rhetoric like Antigone's is a genuine inseparable aspect of the essential function of tragedy: story-telling through poetry. The same is true of another kind of rhetoric or something akin to rhetoric, shown not in reason-patterns of words but in the manipulation of persons. Perhaps this is what Aristotle means by spectacle (ὄψις) but I do not exactly think so.[33] I would call it rather ceremony.

The arrangements of religious ceremony are often used by the story-teller to communicate a scene or story. In *The Odyssey* when the hero visits the shore of the dead he follows the careful instructions given by Circe.[34] He digs his pit, sacrifices the victims so that the blood fills it. One by one the ghosts drink the blood. Critics discuss the religious significance of this ritual, the beliefs that support it, the parallels (or lack of them) elsewhere in literature and recorded practice. Whatever the answers may be to these questions, one thing is clear. The ritual arranges the spirits in a line, so that the hero can interview them one by one. If he were the center of a swarm, the narrative would be unmanageable. Ceremony is used to solve an artist's problem. And it is good theatre; though for the mind's eye, not, like Aristotle's spectacle, the manipulation of visible units.

In our dramatic texts, the lines frequently tell of the placing of persons. In *The Heracleidae*,[35] Euripides has the young sons of Heracles in suppliant posture at the altar through the whole tragedy, though they say nothing. In *Oedipus,* Sophocles has such a solemn entry and departure of silent suppliants at the opening.[36] Or people do and act and instruct each other. The Suppliant Maidens of Aeschylus are told how and where to advance,[37] the family of Ajax what positions to take as preparations are made to carry the body off.[38] Most elaborate of all are the instructions given to Oedipus by the Chorus,, the people of Colonus, in the ritual that will help the gods to tolerate his presence in the land. The details are dwelt on with loving deliberate care while the action waits.[39]

These ceremonies are numerous and not surprising in what was after all a contest under religious sanctions on a religious occasion. Sometimes, again, the performance of ritual with attendant prayer is definitely part of the action in terms of character and motive. Sophocles makes Clytaemestra in his *Electra*, Iocasta in *Oedipus*, come on to perform propitiatory sacrifices to the gods they have been flouting. Iocasta addresses Apollo as "the nearest god" (almost "the handiest") to turn to when things are so bad she is willing to try anything;[40] Clytaemestra offers the same Apollo, in cryptic language, a prayer too immoral in content to be asked straight out (the death of her son).[41] In both cases, the scenes accent the insincerity of the persons, and punctuate the play's progress at the point where the god turns definitely against them. The author may use the gods for his own purposes; his characters, apparently, cannot.

Ceremony, dramatically directed, seems to me to be the essence of three short but complete scenes: the temptation of Agamemnon to the carpet; the uncovering of the dead Clytaemestra by Aegisthus in Sophocles' *Electra*; and the restoration of Alcestis to an Admetus who does not know who she is.

I have spoken earlier about the carpet-scene in *Agamemnon*. It enacts for eye and ear the lyric line dropped in our ears earlier:

> Persuasion the persistent overwhelms him.[42]

At the end of Sophocles' *Electra,* Clytaemestra has been killed, and her covered body lies in sight. Aegisthus enters. He has been told that Orestes is dead, and invited to raise the cloth and look at the body. He does so, sees Clytaemestra and knows in a flash the whole story and his own imminent death. The story could be credibly ended without this ceremony. Aegisthus is alone, unarmed, and unsuspecting. He could simply be struck down. Perhaps it is enough to say: how much less dramatic that would be.[43]

At the end of *Alcestis* when Heracles brings the heroine back from the dead, he goes through an elaborate little ritual of truth-in-lies. He comes on leading a veiled woman. This, he explains, is a girl he has won in a contest,[44] or wrestling match. He insists on handing her over to Admetus; he insists that Admetus shall lead her, personally, into his house; in fact, a remarriage.[45]

Admetus had promised Alcestis the one thing she asked: not to marry again, not to take another woman into his house, her room, her bed.[46] The veiled girl is young, obviously seductive, and reminds him of his lost young wife. She will be irresistible, and Admetus knows it,[47] and struggles to refuse. But he cannot refuse Heracles a favor when Heracles insists. Only when he has taken her hand and effectively agreed to betray Alcestis is he allowed to learn that this is no new woman but his own wife.

My students ask me, what is this scene *for*?

Is it a moralizing ceremony? Admetus has had things very much his own way. For once, the laws of things-as-they-are have been broken, the impossible wish come true. Neither in real life nor in drama is a man often allowed thus to eat his cake and have it too. The man who is given so much must be tested and suffer a few more degrees before he can learn his good fortune properly. He has to learn that his eloquent promises of fidelity were easy to make but hard to keep even for the shortest time.

Or is it pure theatre? Suppose, again, that Heracles simply brought her back and handed her over, with "well, here she is" or however Euripides would say it. That would do Admetus. Will it do us? Admetus, like Bassanio,[48] is gulled before our eyes. It is for us that the scene is played. It is theatre. It plays out the rule of the pattern of the lost one recovered: the lost one, thought to be dead or hopelessly far away, must be right there, unrecognized. What is theatre—like what is poetry—is in the last analysis unanswerable, the escaping dimension. But perhaps Aristotle had a true instinct, and came as close as one can to the answer, when he saw it as misidentification and recognition.[49]

Dianoia, thought, meaning, the grand design, ceremony: they all suggest the final indefinable dimension: the gods. My business has not been to speak of religion as a theme in tragedy. There is no pattern. Nor does any tragic poet have one consistent theology or interpretation of divine will which he puts forward. If they sometimes praise God from the fullness of their hearts, it is hard to know just when they are doing it or just what they are saying. The poets are among other things trying to win prizes in a contest. Religion does not use drama: dramatists use religion. The constantly recurring oracle, soothsaying, or divinely empowered dream is not a design to glorify divinity more than it is a statement of plot. That does not mean that the gods are not in tragedy. They are everywhere in it. Tragedies are the stories of order in the world disordered, and of disorder restored to order. Tragedy goes through patterns of men's actions and wills, but who authorized the patterns? These are the gods, with whom we cannot begin, but with whom, it seems, we always end.

NOTES

I. TRAGEDY AS STORY-TELLING

1. μίμησις πράξεως, *Poetics* 6.2 (1449 b 24). See also 1.2 (1447 a 16–17). For the element of *acting out,* cp. *Poetics* 3.4 (1448 a 26–30). Sophocles is like Homer in that his characters are serious, but like Aristophanes in that they are parts to be acted out, not merely described.

2. *The Poetry of Greek Tragedy.*

3. Summary, Preller-Robert 2.3, pp. 876–7; details arranged and analyzed, pp. 876–968; still further treatment, Robert, *Oidipus.*

4. Nauck, *Fragmenta,* p. 798. The poet is Carcinus.

5. Frag. 541.

6. Aeschylus, Frag. 173; Sophocles, *Oedipus Tyrannus* 733–4.

7. *Odyssey* 11.275–6.

8. See Masqueray, *Sophocle,* vol. 2, pp. 146–50; Kitto, *Greek Tragedy,* pp. 415–16.

9. *The Phoenician Women,* 63–8.

10. *Odyssey* 11.271.

11. See Jebb, *Oedipus at Colonus,* Introduction, pp. xxviii-xxix; Robert, *Oidipus,* pp. 1–47.

12. This is entirely clear from *Antigone* 876–82 and from the course of the action.

13. See Nauck, *Fragmenta,* pp. 404–5. At least two otherwise different versions involved the marriage and the child. See Aristophanes of Byzantium, Sophocles, *Antigone,* Argument and Schol. on 1350; Hyginus, *Fabulae* 72. For Maeon, *Iliad* 4.394, whence Nauck has emended Αἵμονα or Μαίμονα of the mss. to Μαίονα.

14. Sallustius, Argument to Sophocles, *Antigone,* tracing it to Mimnermus, and see further for representations in art Preller-Robert, vol. 2, pp. 924–5.

15. Sallustius, ibid., and see further Preller-Robert, vol. 2, p. 945.

16. Anonymous *Vita* of Sophocles, 21: οἶδε δὲ καιρὸν συμμετρῆσαι καὶ πράγματα, ὥστ᾽ ἐκ μικροῦ ἡμιστιχίου ἢ λέξεως μιᾶς ὅλον ἠθοποιεῖν πρόσωπον.

17. On *hybris* and *nemesis,* see below, Chapter II.

18. Variations of the foundling theme with other recognition-patterns, Menander, *The Hero, The Arbitrators, Periceiromene*; Plautus, *Captives, Epidicus, Poenulus, Truculentus, Rudens*; Terence, *Andria*; etc.

19. Sophocles, Fragments 589–608 Nauck; 648–69 Pearson.

20. Sophocles, Fragments 89–96 Nauck; 92–100 Pearson, with notes ("we are not in a position to distinguish the treatment of Euripides from that of Sophocles," p. 58). See also *Ion* and/or *Creusa* (the same play, and the same plot as in Euripides?), Fragments 319–20 and 350–9 Pearson; *Aleadae*, Fragments 74–88 Nauck; 77–91 Pearson.

21. Euripides, Fragments (Nauck): *Alexander* (42–64); *Alope* (105–13); *Antigone* (probably; 157–78); *Antiope* (179–227, and for new fragments, pp. 60–70 Page); *Auge* (265–81); *Melanippe* (two plays, 480–513 plus pp. 108–19 Page).

22. Hesiod, *Theogony* 468–86.

23. Matthew 2.3–15.

24. Sophocles, *Electra* 11–14; Euripides, *Electra* 16–18; 556.

25. Euripides, *Cresphontes*, Fragments 449–59 Nauck. On the found-ling-story, see Freud, *Moses and Monotheism*, pp. 7–17. But Freud has warped the outlines to fit his prejudices, e.g. (p. 9): "When full grown he rediscovers his noble parents after many strange adventures, *wreaks vengeance on his father*, and, recognized by his people, attains fame and greatness." (My italics.) Only Oedipus "wreaks vengeance on his father," and that by accident, since, in Sophocles at least, that is exactly what he does not want to do. Often a usurper or stepfather is punished. Freud further fails to connect the foundling with the other types of missing person, as well as ignoring the girl-foundlings. In general, I think, he would scarcely have considered the claims of story-telling for its own sake.

26. Euripides, *Helen* 132; 204; 279; 290, etc.

27. Euripides, *Iphigeneia in Tauris* 56; 564.

28. Ibid. 467–71, etc.

29. See above, note 25.

30. Euripides, *Ion* 774–95 and action following.

31. Eugammon, *Telegony*, in the summary of Proclus. See Kinkel, *Epicorum Graecorum Fragmenta*, pp. 57–9; Evelyn-White, *Hesiod*, pp. 530–2; Sophocles, *Odysseus Acanthoplex* or *Niptra*, Fragments 415–29 Nauck; 453–61 Pearson.

32. Aristotle, *Poetics* 13.5 (1453a 8–23); Else, *Aristotle's Poetics ad*

loc. (pp. 376–99). For a consideration of the use of ἁμαρτία and cog-nates in tragedy itself, see Harsh, "Ἁμαρτία again," *TAPA* 76 (1945), pp. 47–58 and especially pp. 53–6. In the form ἁμαρτία, an *act*, not a trait, is always meant. Further full literature in Else. Note particularly Else's discussion of this kind of *hamartia* in connection with the stories of heroic houses cited by Aristotle, that is, those of Alcmeon, Oedipus, Orestes, Meleager, Thyestes, and Telephus.

33. Thus the Euripidean "omniscient" prologue (spoken by a god) tends explicitly to put the audience on a semidivine level above the struggling and deceived persons of the play. The practice is often fol-lowed in new comedy: a striking example is the concept-goddess Agnoia in Menander's *Periceiromene* (though she is not technically a pro-logue). The divine prologue's complement, the "god from the machine," brings the play's persons up to our level, while often further enlightening us.

34. Exceptions include Euripides, *Ion,* and Sophocles, *Antigone.*

In *Ion,* Xuthus will be left ignorant of the secret known to the other principals, the Chorus, the gods, and us.

In *Antigone,* the heroine must be supposed to believe that Haemon has deserted her when in fact he has not. Since critics generally ignore this point, two statements are worth making concerning Antigone and Haemon.

(1) Reading 568–70 in the most natural sense Ismene attests mutual love between Antigone and Haemon.

Unless ἡρμοσμένα has more implications than I think, Ismene is as reserved in her language as Creon is brutal, but she still is saying that things between them are very close, and that should be enough. Whit-man, *Sophocles,* p. 86 remarks: "Ismene intimates that Antigone and Haemon are made for each other, but it is hard to believe her." But *why* is it hard? (Masqueray translated 570 "Ce n'était pas ce qui etait convenu entre lui et elle," defensible but requiring a very strained ὡς=οὕτως).

Then at 795–8, when the chorus says

νικᾷ δ' ἐναργὴς βλεφάρων
ἵμερος εὐλέκτρου
νύμφας

ἵμερος must refer to the bride as well as to her admirer or the passage is untranslatable (note that Jebb's "victorious is the love-kindling light from the eyes of the fair bride" does *not* translate it).

Finally, there is no escaping the bridal imagery through 781–882, much of it spoken by Antigone. Waldock, *Sophocles,* p. 109, note 2 would dispose of this with: "We can make far too much of Antigone's laments that she will never know the married state. They are in large part conventional for one in her situation. Compare Macaria." But he is not playing fair by his own rules (that we should take what Sophocles gives us, rather than conclude what he might or ought to have been intending).

(2) Even granting that Antigone is (for all we know) not nearly so deep in love with Haemon as he with her, she is plainly bitter about the absence of all φίλοι in her time of need (847, 876, 881–2) and the φίλος conspicuously absent is Haemon.

It is of course true that the love-story is a subtheme in *Antigone.* Perhaps she dies unenlightened because she must go all the way unsupported, so far as she knows, except by Ismene, whom she found inadequate.

35. See Murray, *Excursus,* p. 341. note 1: "It is worth remarking that the year-Daimon has equally left its mark on the new comedy. The somewhat tiresome foundling of unknown parentage who grows up, is recognized, and inherits, in almost every play of Menander that is known to us, is clearly descended from the foundling of Euripidean tragedy who turns out to be the son of a god and inherits a kingdom. And that foundling in turn is derived from the year-Baby who grows up in such miraculous fashion in the Mummer's play." Some of these derivations are doubtless sound, but the whole sweeping assertion ignores the foundling as a piece of story-material offered by real life.

36. 'Ο Ἀφέντης Πολυρόβιθας. I have followed the version of Maria Lioudaki, Στοῦ Πάππου τὰ Γόνατα, pp. 94–100.

37. In some versions, as I understand, the little old man is the Παγκράτωρ, that is, Christ himself.

38. See Stith Thompson, *Motive–Index,* Ind. Stud. 101, p. 283.

39. As applied to tragedy, the term "happy ending" is somewhat variable and misleading. The connected trilogy of Aeschylus seems generally to end in reconciliation, but not always (*Seven Against Thebes*). If we apply the simple Aristotelian μεταβολή ἐξ εὐτυχίας εἰς δυστυχίαν and vice versa (*Poetics* 13.2=1452b35), *Agamemnon* and *Libation Bearers* are "unhappy," but *Eumenides* is "happy." In these same terms, of the extant tragedies of Sophocles, not only *Philoctetes* but *Electra* will end

"happily." *Oedipus at Colonus* can scarcely be classified as moving in either direction. Of the extant plays of Euripides, *Alcestis, Heraclidae, Ion, Iphigeneia in Tauris, Helen, Orestes,* and *Iphigeneia in Aulis* (original ending lost) end "happily." Aristotle's preference for ἐξ εὐτυχίας εἰς δυστυχίαν is no doubt responsible for the general modern association of tragedy with unhappy endings.

40. On the Sphinx, see Robert, *Oidipus,* pp. 48–58.

41. Orwell, *Dickens, Dali and Others,* pp. 52–6. Note, for instance, pp. 52–3: "When Martin Chuzzlewit had made it up with his uncle, when Nicholas Nickleby had married money, when John Harmon had been enriched by Boffin—what did they do? The answer evidently is that they did nothing"; or, p. 55: "The ideal to be striven for then, appears to be something like this: a hundred thousand pounds, a quaint old house with plenty of ivy on it, a sweetly womanly wife, a horde of children, and no work." *Mutatis mutandis,* that is where we leave the effendi.

42. *The Poetry of Greek Tragedy.*

43. *Peace* 50–81. The most elaborate and advanced plot of this sort is perhaps to be found in *The Birds,* where Pisthetaerus, with the birds' help, succeeds in blockading and starving out the gods of the sky.

44. One reservation should, however, be made. While folk-tales abound in kings, queens, princes, and princesses, the king in this story is, as usually happens, imagined as nothing but a very rich peasant.

45. *Odyssey* 13.291 9; 330–8.

46. Folk-tale as proto-tragedy may be seen on a more serious plane in the Greek ballad of "The Bridge at Arta" (I have translated it in my *Poems,* pp. 65–8). The great bridge which was being built kept collapsing. A little bird told the workmen that a human sacrifice was necessary, and hinted at the master-mason's beautiful wife. The master-mason tried to deprecate this course of events, but the bird told her to go visit the workmen at the bridge. When she came, her husband tricked her into going down inside the unfinished pier; and he and the rest threw down rubble and stones to seal her within the bridge. (In modern Athens, I am told, no new house is built without being consecrated by the blood of a chicken.) The story of human sacrifice is a pattern of tragedy, and this ballad, of 92 lines, could be the outline of a tragedy. But the pattern so dominates that it dispenses entirely with human motivation, substituting miracle, so that there is no character. (It is true that Aristotle

(*Poetics* 6.14=1450 a 24) says that there *can* be tragedy without character.)

47. *Poetics* 6.27–1450 b 16.

48. See, for instance, E. R. Dodds, Introduction to Euripides, *Bacchae*. p. xli: "As the 'moral' of the *Hippolytus* is that sex is a thing about which you cannot afford to make mistakes, so the 'moral' of the *Bacchae* is that we ignore at our peril the demand of the human spirit for Dionysiac experience." I take Professor Dodd's quotation marks to mean that these morals are not sufficient definitions of the plays in question.

49. See Pohlenz, *Die Griechische Tragödie*, esp. p. 42: ". . . der Kunstler Aischylos ist zugleich und zuerst der religiose Denker und Prophet." On Sophocles, p. 162: "Wie Aischylos fühlte er sich nicht nur als Dichter, sondern als der Erzieher seines Volkes"; and on Euripides, p. 468: "Der Dichter Euripides . . . ist zugleich der Volkserzieher." See also E. Meyer, *Geschichte des Altertums*,2 v. 4, p. 151. Such views are supported by Aristophanes, *Frogs* 1008–12. But is Aristophanes, who himself always had a message, authorized to speak for the intentions of Aeschylus, or even Euripides (Sophocles he barely mentions)?

50. For Aeschylus, I think of *Agamemnon* 338–47. Clytaemestra is speaking, out of character. I now am inclined to think that she speaks for the author. *Agamemnon* 838–40 is perhaps dramatic irony. For Sophocles, *Antigone* 332–75 is thinly attached to the situation, and the content of *Oedipus at Colonus* 1211–38 is not quite accounted for by 1239–48. See also *Antigone* 872–5. Euripides offers the best cases of counter-dramatic moralizing, for instance, Hecuba's outbursts on divine justice, *Trojan Women* 884–8. The *dike* in this play (*a*) is the work of personified gods, and (*b*) will not apply to Helen. So too, *Heracles* 1340–6 (styled a *parergon*; author's parenthesis?) contradicts previously staged action. In Greek tragedy, one must always infer the intention. The tragic poet lacks alike the *parabasis* of the Athenian comic poet and the preface of the modern playwright.

51. See the conclusions of Aeschylus, *Eumenides*, and Sophocles, *Antigone*, discussed in the text; also, Sophocles, *Oedipus Tyrannus* (but lines 1524–30, which will not construe as they read, have often been damned as a whole or in part), *Ajax*, *Women of Trachis* (too brutal for some modern tastes); Euripides, *Alcestis* (cf. *Medea*, *Andromache*, *Helen*, *Bacchae*), *Heracles*, *Ion*. More explicit moralization may be contained in the *deus ex machina* scene.

52. *Philoctetes* 902–3. See below, p. 45.

II. PATTERNS OF TRAGIC NARRATIVE

1. 13.5=1453a.

2. See Chapter I, note 32.

3. Note that Aristotle says, or seems to say, that the *best* kind of tragedy is to be found in a kind of situation nowadays mostly assigned to melodrama or romantic comedy. See *Poetics*, 14.19=1454a: "Finally, there is the best kind of all, I mean as where in *Cresphontes* Merope is about to kill her son, but does not kill him, but recognizes him, and so too in *Iphigeneia* with sister and brother, and in *Helle* the son about to betray (? sell off?) his mother recognizes her."

4. *Poetics* 15.11 – 1454b.

5. Viz.: Aeschylus, *The Suppliant Maidens, The Libation Bearers, The Eumenides*; Sophocles, *Electra*; Euripides, *The Heracleidae, Andromache, The Suppliant Women, Ion, The Trojan Women, Electra, Iphigeneia in Tauris, Helen, The Phoenician Women, Orestes, Iphigeneia in Aulis.*

6. These ten, which follow, may merit brief discussion.

Aeschylus, *The Seven Against Thebes.* The fault of Eteocles, if he is meant to have one, is not the decisive cause of his catastrophe, which does not affect him alone. Thebes, in fact, is saved, which was what he wanted. Other themes which might be emphasized, such as willing self-sacrifice, paternal curse, fate, or tragic pattern, overlie and seem to bury any master-pattern of flaw.

Prometheus. This is not the story of the hero's downfall, but a part of his story of suffering tending toward ultimate release and reconciliation. To some extent this is willing self-sacrifice. The ἁμαρτία of 261–8 can only be from the point of view of self-advantage.

Agamemnon. I find it hard to identify the flaw in a noble nature (questionable) which led to his downfall. A revenge-drama, constantly leading into larger issues?

Sophocles, *The Women of Trachis.* Flaws in Heracles and Deianeira may be inferred from the text. The active ingredient is, for Heracles, his whole nature; for Deianeira, the fatal choice (*hamartia* in that sense?).

Euripides, *Alcestis.* It is easy to find the flaw in Admetus, but it did not permanently destroy anyone.

Hecuba. This seems to represent the deterioration of a whole nature through ill-treatment. The revenge-play cannot seem to be well accounted for by the *hamartia*-pattern.

Medea. Somewhat similar. The fault is there but brings about the triumph of Medea, not her downfall.

Heracles. Euripides tries as hard as he can to knock it into our heads that the motivation is external. If we insist on reading it otherwise, that is our own doing.

The Bacchae. The extent to which Dionysus secures his revenge and vindication by exploiting an inner weakness in Pentheus may be, and has been, disputed. To me, Pentheus seems never to initiate action, but to *react* to external pressures of appalling force.

Rhesus. This may not be by Euripides, but there is no evidence that it is not a fifth-century tragedy. Analysis is difficult. Who is the hero? If Rhesus, he has the fault of overconfidence, but it does not *motivate* his destruction, which looks like an accident. If Hector, over-confidence is combined with sober courage, and it is not clear to me what the poet means or wants us to think of him. His catastrophe lies outside the play, in the *Iliad,* which the spectator can hardly ignore at the end.

7. See below, Chapter III, pp. 50-2.

8. *Ajax* 758-61.

9. 470-2.

10. 690-2.

11. *Antigone* 471-2.

δηλοῖ τὸ γοῦν λῆμ' ὠμὸν ἐξ ὠμοῦ πατρὸς
τῆς παιδός· εἴκειν δ' οὐκ ἐπίσταται κακοῖς.

For ὠμός Jebb's "passionate" is surprising and poor. ὠμός can mean "fierce," but in this context plainly means "unyielding."

12. *Philoctetes* 1316-23.

13. *Oedipus at Colonus* 855.

14. 1192-8.

15. Homer, *Iliad* 24.601-9.

16. Herodotus 1.34.1.

17. Essential meanings in Liddell and Scott, who ignore any particular connection with the behavior of man toward god or gods. Boisacq, *Dictionnaire Etymologique*[3], connects with Briaros and ideas of violence.

18. Demosthenes 21 (*Against Meidias*), *passim*; the text of the Athenian *nomos* is given, ibid., 47. So throughout the orators, and the basic sense in Athenian law. For this sense in tragedy, Euripides, *Bacchae* 9; *Cyclops*

665 (the blinding of Polyphemus); *Hippolytus* 445–6 where the text is worth quoting:

ὃν δ' ἂν περισσὸν καὶ φρονοῦνθ' εὕρῃ μέγα,

τοῦτον λαβοῦσα — πῶς δοκεῖς; — καθύβρισεν.

Thus here the mortal who is περισσός, who is guilty of μέγα φρονεῖν, is the victim of ὕβρις on the part of the god. In Sophocles, *Women of Trachis* 280, the term seems to mean "foul play"; at 888 it refers to Deianeira's suicide ("ghastly act" or "self-violence"). In Euripides, *Orestes* 1038, it is "murder."

19. Gorgias, *Helen* 7; Euripides, *Hippolytus* 1073; *Ion* 506; Demosthenes 19.309.

20. Sophocles, *Women of Trachis* 280.

21. *Acts* 27.10, 21 of the *beating* taken by a ship in a storm (Vulgate, *iniuria*, as Latin for ὕβρις also Goetz, *Thesaurus* s.v.); as shipwreck (?), the anonymous lyric fragment sometimes attributed to Simonides (fragment 42 Diehl), see Edmonds, *Lyra Graeca*, vol. 3, p. 472; so too perhaps Pindar, *Pythia* 1.72; Aeschylus, *Seven* 406; perhaps Euripides, *Rhesus* 500 (the *damage* done by Odysseus).

22. Herodotus 4.129.2 of donkeys braying, compare Pindar, *Pythia* 10.36; Euripides, *Bacchae* 743 (of a bull; "ramping"?); Herodotus 1.189.1 of a bolting horse, caught and swept away by the *violence* of the river, 1.189.2; compare the river Hybristes, Aeschylus, *Prometheus* 717, and Sir John Mandeville, p. 201, "and by the rivers may no man go. For the water runneth so rudely and so sharply, because that it cometh down so outrageously from the high places above. . . ." For sheer wild spirits of men, Herodotus 1.89.2; 2.32.3.

23. This seems to be the main sense in *The Iliad*, 1.203,214 (Agamemnon's rapacity toward Achilles); see 13.633, Menelaus on the *insatiable* Trojans (here first with *koros*; *hybris-koros*="greed"—"glut"?). See Pindar, *Olympia* 13.10; Theognis 751; and in particular, Solon 3.7–10; 5.9–10. In Solon, it is hard or impossible to distinguish greedy from criminal behavior, but the greed alike of the haves and the have-nots seems to be his special preoccupation. See also *The Odyssey* 14.262; 17.245. Herodotus 7.16a2 indicates greed on a grand national scale. This particular sense is rare in tragedy, but see Euripides, *Phoenician Women* 620.

24. Best seen in Aeschylus, *Suppliant Maidens,* where the variants of *hybris* appear ten times, always in connection wtih the Egyptians (in the last two cases, 880, 881, apparently with their herald, but the reading is

doubtful) and referring to their wildly amorous pursuit of the maidens. The length to which modern misapplication can go is well illustrated in a recent note on this play; see H. Spier, *Classical Journal* 57 (1962), p. 316: "One may argue that they (sc. The Maidens) have one frequent attribute of the protagonists: hubris [Miss Spier's preferred spelling]. Their hubris is their claim to virginity." Elsewhere, it is hard to distinguish this sense from the application to general misbehavior and disorder (*hybris* in Xenophanes 1.17 seems to imply "drunk and disorderly"). *Hybristes* applied to the Centaurs, Sophocles, *Women of Trachis* 1096, would probably hint at their lustfulness; so Plato makes Alcibiades use the term while comparing him to a satyr, *Symposium* 215b. Lustfulness is a plain meaning in Pindar, *Pythia* 2.28 and lustful action in Herodotus 6.137.3. In Euripides, *Bacchae,* the term describes general disorderliness or wildness in which a taint of sex is suspected (247,779). In *The Trojan Women* 997, 1020 he seems in an interesting way to combine the early (*NED,* first meaning) with the later sense of the English word "luxury."

25. In *The Trojan Women* 69 both Athene and her temple are said by her to have suffered violence (ὑβρισθεῖσαν) from Ajax Oileus (violation of sanctuary, attempted violation of Cassandra). This approaches the "modern" meaning, but denotes vigorous physical action, not mere pride, arrogance, or complacency. For "violence" more generally, see for instance Aeschylus, *Seven Against Thebes* 502; Sophocles, *Ajax* 1060, 1088; *Oedipus at Colonus* 883; Euripides, *Ion* 810; *Bacchae* 555, 1297; *Iphigeneia in Aulis* 961.

26. An important meaning. At Athens, accused and accuser stood, respectively, on the two rocks of ὕβρις and ἀναίδεια, Pausanias 1.28.5; not "insolence" and "recklessness" (Bury and Meiggs, *History of Greece,* p. 173) but better "injury and ruthlessness" (Frazer; *contumelia et impudentia,* Cicero, *de Legibus* 2.11.18) or simply "crime and vindictiveness" (for ἀναίδεια Liddell and Scott give "unforgivingness"; compare the λᾶας ἀναιδής of *Iliad* 4.521). Aeschylus contrasts *hybris* with *dike, Agamemnon* 763, and Homer with *eunomia, Odyssey* 17.485–7, where it is said (by the Suitors!) that the gods, disguised as visiting strangers, go about the world inspecting the *hybris* and *eunomia* of men. Solon makes *hybris* rather, perhaps, the greedy violence that produces or results from lawlessness and crime (1.11); elsewhere he lines it up with other terms of moral disapproval, *koros, ate,* crooked judgments, ambitious action, quarrelsome politics and rivalry (3.34–9) as properties of *dys-*

nomia. In such a context, *hybris* has no specific technical meaning that can be pressed. Hesiod opposes *hybris* to *dike* as if *hybris* and *adikia* were synonymous (*Works and Days* 213–14), which they come close to being, but as usual *hybris* is less precise, more variable. In Bacchylides 14.57–63 ὕβρις might be translated "violence," "lawlessness," "lust," or "rapacity" but not (Edmonds) "presumptuousness." For the sense of "crime," see again Herodotus 1.100.2 (the duty of the judge is to suppress anyone committing *hybris*), and see also Theognis 40, 1103; Pindar, *Isthmia* 4.8–9. See Euripides, *Orestes* 1642, for the disorder and criminality of the world to be cleaned out by Zeus.

27. *Paradise Lost* 1.501–2, but see the whole passage on Belial, 490–505. I have little doubt that Milton was thinking of *hybris*. He pictures bullies swaggering in the streets with violence, especially lustful violence; note the words "lewd," "vice," "lust," "violence," "luxurious" (see above, note 24), "riot," "injury," "outrage," "Sodom," "rape."

The Suitors of *The Odyssey* deserve special notice as a group regularly accused of *hybris* (1.227, 368; 3.207; 4.627; 15.329; 16.86, 410, 418; 17.581, 588; 18.381; 20.170, 370; 23.64; 24.352 are instances) which characterizes their entire behavior in the house of Odysseus. They are proud (ἀγήνορες, 1.44, a term which can be applied to approved heroes) but that is only part of it. They crash the house of their absent host uninvited, try to marry his wife, eat up his substance, drink hard, bully the household, plot against the life of the son and heir, have love-thoughts about Penelope and seduce the maids when they can. They at no time, however, challenge or speak disrespectfully toward the gods, but are careful in their attitude toward them (16.400–6; 17.481.7; 20.240–6).

28. For a definition of this sense, see Aristotle, *Rhetoric* 2.1378b 23–5: ἔστι γὰρ ὕβρις τὸ πράττειν καὶ λέγειν ἐφ' οἶς αἰσχύνη ἔστι τῷ πάσχοντι, μὴ ἵνα τι γίγνηται αὐτῷ ἄλλο ἢ ὃ τι ἐγένετο ἀλλ' ὅπως ἡσθῇ, that is, shaming of the victim in word and act, for the pleasure of it. This is the spirit of the so-called *Scolium* of Hybrias the Cretan, Diehl, vol. 2, p. 128; see Bowra, *Greek Lyric Poetry,* pp. 437–43. Abuse of power is the commonest single sense of *hybris* in tragedy. It is probably the sense of that mysterious line, Aeschylus, *Prometheus* 970: οὕτως ὑβρίζειν τοὺς ὑβρίζοντας χρεών, and certainly of *Agamemnon* 1612 (of Aegisthus). Euripides in his *Electra* uses *hybris* or variants nine times, and chiefly or always in this sense, though not always applied to Aegisthus,

and applies it to Eurystheus's maltreatment of Heracles or the Heracleidae, *Heracleidae* 18, 457, 947, 948, to Lycus's abuse of Heracles and his family, *Hercules Furens* 313, 459, 708, 741. For this sense, see also Sophocles, *Ajax* 196, 590; *Electra* 293, 522–3; *Philoctetes* 342, 397; Euripides, *Medea* 255, 603, 782; *Suppliant Women* 512, 743. Such abuse can apply to the dead, and those who try to protect them, Sophocles, *Ajax* 1093, 1151, 1358; *Electra* 271 (combined with lustful and generally outrageous behavior); Euripides, *Medea* 1380. Abuse of power characterizes the tyrant, Herodotus 3.80.2–3.

29. In Sophocles, *Electra* 881, Chrysothemis disclaims *mockery*; she has no power to abuse, merely security. So in the same play Clytaemestra is accused of mocking the dead, not of physical abuse, 790, 794, thereby risking the *nemesis* (resentment) of the dead. See Euripides, *Orestes* 1581. Euripides, *Bacchae* 616 (Dionysus, who has bewildered Pentheus) seems to mean either "I had my fun with him" or "I made a fool of him" ("That was just (*kai*) the laugh I had against him," Dodds). In Plato, *Symposium* 175E ὑβρίστης εἶ, seems to mean "you're making fun of me."

30. See, again, the crucial passage of Herodotus, 3.80–2. Against the *hybris* of the irresponsible tyrant like Cambyses is set the *hybris* of the irresponsible mob, 3.81.1–2. Menelaus and Agamemnon are charged with abuse of power over the dead Ajax, Sophocles, *Ajax* 1093, 1151, 1385 (see above, note 28); their charge against Ajax and his brother is *hybris* as mutiny or insubordination, 1081, 1088, 1151. So, too, Creon of Antigone, *Antigone* 480–2. See also Aeschylus, *Prometheus* 82. Phaedra's nurse tells her that to resist love is *hybris* (insubordination), Euripides, *Hippolytus* 474, though the term is not used for Hippolytus's more explicit challenge.

31. Antigone had acted rebelliously, as well as speaking insolently. In *Electra* 613, Electra has merely spoken disrespectfully to her mother. Compare Euripides, *Alcestis* 679. In *The Phoenician Women* 179 ἐφυβρίζει refers to the mere threats of Capaneus, while at 1112 Amphiaraus disdains vainglorious devices for his shield. At *Bacchae* 1311, 1347 ὑβρίζειν means "treat without proper respect." In the second of these cases, the god complains of his treatment by his mortal cousin.

32. *Iliad* 24.602–17; for the *Niobe* of Aeschylus, see Nauck, *Fragmenta*, pp. 50–5 and in particular the papyrus fragment, Page, *Greek Literary Papyri*, pp. 3–9, where the nature of the offense is precisely stated. See lines 15–19:

... θεὸς μὲν αἰτίαν φύει β[ροτοῖς
ὅταν κα]κῶσαι δῶμα παμπήδη[ν θέληι·
τέως δ]ὲ θνητὸν ὄντα χρὴ τὸν ἐ[κ θεῶν
ὄλβον π]εριοτέλλοντα μὴ θρασυστομ[εῖν.
οἱ δ'αἰὲν] εὖ πράσσντες οὔποτ' ἤλπισαν ...

Lines 1–2 are guaranteed from Plato, *Republic* 380a. See also Apollodorus, *Library* 3.5.6 with Frazer's notes and references to later authors.

33. Sophocles, *Ajax,* where the nature of the offence is specified and general conclusions drawn, 127–33; 756–77. The omission of ὕβρις here is the more notable in that the word, in one form or another, occurs fourteen times in this play.

34. *Odyssey* 4.499–510. On the other hand, Euripides does make Athene complain of *hybris* committed against her by Ajax, *Trojan Women* 69; not a challenge or boast, but actual violation of the temple and lustful assault against Cassandra.

35. *Iliad* 2.594–600. This challenge does, however, seem to be called *hybris* in Euripides, *Rhesus* 917, though the context connects this *hybris* with the sex act of the river Strymon against the Muse. This seems to be the only case in tragedy where the term is applied to a boast or challenge against the gods (*Rhesus* may not be by Euripides, but I do not know of any actual evidence that it is not a fifth-century tragedy).

36. *Odyssey* 8.224–8.

37. The nature of his offence is fully stated, Euripides, *Hippolytus* 1–23; 88–120. Among various other "*hybris*-substitutes," Hippolytus is here characterized as σεμνός.

38. Their story is told at length, Bacchylides 10.40–112. See also Apollodorus, *Library* 2.2.2, with Frazer's notes.

39. See J. E. Harry on Aeschylus, *Prometheus* 970. "Prometheus is not in a position to ὑβρίζειν."

40. Aeschylus, *Persians* 745–50; 807–22.

41. Neither "pride" nor "arrogance" is attested in Liddell and Scott.

42. ἐλπίζω is used of Croesus eight times, ἐλπίς once. Herodotus never speaks of ὕβρις in connection with Croesus.

43. Herodotus 1.34.1.

44. See Liddell and Scott, s.v. "properly, like νέμησις, *distribution of what is due.*" Despite this, I find the further definition self-contradictory, viz.: "but in usage always *retribution, esp. righteous anger* aroused by injustice," etc. Anger is not retribution. In Homer, νέμεσις plus the verbs

νεμεσῶ, νεμεσίζομαι, etc., regularly stands for the feeling of moral indignation. As Liddell and Scott observe, it is not there used of the gods. In Hesiod, *Works and Days* 197-201, Aidos and Nemesis abandon communities which are hopelessly corrupt. As *aidos* is the inner feeling whose presence prevents outrageous action, so her sister *nemesis* would be the public conscience, the feeling of others against the wrongdoers.

In the extant corpus of tragedy the word appears just ten times with νεμεσητός once. They are: Aeschylus, *Seven* 235; Fragment 266.4-5; Sophocles, *Electra* 792, 1467; *Philoctetes* 518, 602, with 1193; *Oedipus at Colonus* 1753; Euripides, *The Phoenician Women* 182; *Orestes* 1362; Fragment 1040. In all cases, "resentment," "anger," "indignation," are possible translations. In Sophocles, *Philoctetes* 518, Euripides, *Orestes* 1362, *The Phoenician Women* 182, and Fragment 1040 the terms could also, but need not be, translated as "punishment" or "retribution."

45. This is the regular sense in Homer.

46. Sophocles, *Philoctetes* 518, 602; Euripides, *The Phoenician Women* 182; *Orestes* 1362. In Sophocles, *Electra* 1467-8 it is coupled with φθόνος (of the gods? But they are not in the text, though Masqueray translates as if they were).

47. Aeschylus, Fragment 266; Sophocles, *Electra* 792.

48. On this, see Farnell, *Cults of the Greek States,* vol. 2, pp. 487-98, with the pertinent material assembled in the notes.

49. Such as is made by Farnell, op. cit., p. 495: ". . . the goddess who feels righteous indignation at evil acts and evil words, and hence, by a natural transition, as the goddess who punishes man for these." The transition is indeed natural but if hastily applied may lead to misconception and mistranslation.

50. See above, note 44. *The New English Dictionary* defines Nemesis as "the goddess of just retribution, who brings down all immoderate good fortune, checks the presumption that attends it . . . and is the punisher of extraordinary crimes." I would note that, while the modern student, even the scholar, habitually thinks of *hybris* as a feeling or state of mind and *nemesis* as a kind of activity, the ancient evidence rather indicates the reverse.

51. Pausanias 1.33.2.

52. The idea of *hybris* as pride or arrogance punished by the gods was perhaps first clearly stated by K. Lehrs in a pair of essays entitled "Neid der Gotter" and "Veberhebung (Hybris)" which seem to have

appeared first in 1838. See Lehrs, *Populäre Aufsätze*, pp. 35-70. I have not been able to trace this notion to any earlier work, but it is difficult to document a negative fact. Among recent works which deal with *hybris* in tragedy and elsewhere, one might mention Del Grande, *Hybris*. Del Grande begins (p. 1) by defining *hybris* as "tracotanza" (that is, English "arrogance" according to three Italian-English dictionaries) which directly offends the gods and thus encounters *Nemesis* ("impersonale divina vendetta"). The monograph is confusing in that it is a study at once of the Greek word ὕβρις, including the impersonal senses of Attic law, and of what might be called the modern concept of a *hybris*-situation, defined above, where the Greek word generally does not appear. In essence, Del Grande's concept repeats that of Lehrs, which has been adopted *a priori* by many writers, both technical and popular, on Greek tragedy and Greek thought in general.

53. Perhaps one should note also *Hippolytus* and *The Bacchae* of Euripides, more complex actions to be discussed later.

54. For *Niobe,* see below, p. 27; the fragments of *Thamyras* and *Ajax Locrius* provide no evidence.

55. *Poetics* 18.15.

56. At least as treated by Aeschylus. See *Frogs* 911-20.

57. Euripides, *The Bacchae* 9.

58. Euripides, *Hippolytus* 445-6:

ὃν δ'ἂν περισσὸν καὶ φρονοῦνθ' εὕρῃ μέγα,

τοῦτον λαβοῦσα — πῶς δοκεῖς; — καθύβρισεν.

Here the goddess acts in ὕβρις against the mortal, guilty of *hybris* in the modern sense (note "*hybris*-substitutes" in line 445).

59. *Agamemnon* 456-74. In *Electra,* Sophocles makes it a boast by Agamemnon which offended Artemis and forced the sacrifice of Iphigeneia, 566-72. Plainly I think for Sophocles, what is required or given fact is the anger of Artemis. Any good *reason* will do.

60. See Dodds, Introduction to *The Bacchae,* p. xliii: "in his [sc. Euripides'] revenge plays—*Medea, Hecuba, Electra*—the spectator's sympathy is first enlisted for the avenger and then made to extend to the avenger's victims."

61. Stesichorus, Fragment 17.

62. *Iliad* 9.532-40, cp. Bacchylides, 5.97-110; Sophocles, Fragment 369, cited, Lucian, *Symposium* 25; Euripides, Fragment 516 (Aristophanes, Frogs 1238). Many stories of divine jealousy are incorporated in

the *Metamorphoses* of Ovid, as for instance the tales of Ocyrhoe (2.634–675), Arachne (6.1–145), Niobe (6.146–312), Marsyas (6.382–400), Chione (11.291–345), Anaxarete (14.698–771).

63. For Lycurgus, see Homer, *Iliad* 6.130–40; the fragments of Aeschylus, *Lycurgeia* tetralogy (*Edoni, Bassarae, Neanisci, Lycurgus*); Sophocles, *Antigone* 955–65. For Pentheus, Euripides, *Bacchae*; Aeschylus, fragments of *Pentheus*; *Eumenides* 26.

64. Euripides, *Bacchae* 1344–9; 1374–8.

65. Page, *Greek Literary Papyri*, p. 8.

66. *Republic* 2.380a.

67. *Republic* 10.617d–e.

68. Herodotus 1.8–13.

69. Herodotus 1.8.1. In saying "the story" demands this pattern of choice, I mean the story as told by Herodotus. Nicolaus of Damascus has a different version, Fragment 47.1–11 Jacoby. See How and Wells, *Commentary on Herodotus,* Appendix 1.9, pp. 374–5. The story as told by Herodotus was evidently used in a tragedy of uncertain date and origin; see the fragment of trimeters first published by Lobel, *Proceedings of the British Academy* 35 (1950), pp. 1–12; see also D. L. Page, *A New Chapter in the History of Greek Tragedy.* How would the queen, in the case of Gyges' refusal, have secured his execution? One might conjecture, by a trumped-up story that he had made advances to her, with a view to murdering Candaules and securing the throne. Compare what Antaea says to Proetus in the story of Bellerophon as told by Homer, *Iliad* 6.164–5:

> τεθναίης, ὦ Προῖτ', ἢ κάκτανε Βελλεροφόντην,
> ὅς μ'ἔθελεν φιλότητι μιγήμεναι οὐκ ἐθελούσῃ.

70. As in 1.8–13 the full conversations, the detail of the disrobing scene with the clothes "laid one by one on the chair," etc.

71. Herodotus 6.109,3.

72. Herodotus 8.57–8.

73. Compare the choice of the Persians, 1.126; a different choice, 9.122; the choice of Xerxes, fully dramatized, 7.8–11; of a rather different sort, the choice of the wife of Intaphrenes, 3.119.3–7. One thinks of the two destinies open to Achilles, *Iliad* 9.411–16.

74. Xenophon, *Memorabilia* 2.1.21–34. Just before this, Xenophon makes Socrates quote Hesiod, *Works and Days* 287–92, which may indeed have inspired the parable of Prodicus.

75. *Essai sur le tragique d'Euripide,* p. 33.

76. 672-3.

77. 1375-6.

78. Aeschylus, *Eumenides* 735.

79. *Eumenides* 752-3.

80. 899–903. I have quoted my own translation, and, though "be shamed" is hardly satisfactory for αἰδεσθῶ, I find improvement difficult. For *aidos* as the inner twin to outer nemesis, see above, note 44.

81. Sophocles, *Antigone* 37-43.

82. 555.

83. Sophocles, *Ajax* 470-2.

84. 690-2.

85. Perhaps I may here refer to my own discussion of this deception, *The Poetry of Greek Tragedy,* pp. 68-74.

86. This is evident from 141-52.

87. *The Women of Trachis* 582-97.

88. Here see Dodds, Introduction to *The Bacchae,* p. xlvi: "He [sc. Euripides] shows us . . . in the *Heracles* the splendor of bodily strength and courage toppling over into megalomania and madness." This is attractive but misleading. We may so infer the meaning, but this is not what Euripides shows us. What he shows us is the goddess Lyssa driving a sane man mad, *Heracles* 822-73, especially 833-7; 859-66.

89. Euripides, *Andromache* 404-20.

90. Euripides, *Iphigeneia in Aulis* 1375-6; Macaria in *The Heracleidae* 500-2; Menoeceus in *The Phoenician Women* 991-8.

91. 1348-53.

III. PATTERNS OF CHOICE, REVENGE AND TRAGEDY

1. See above, p. 29.

2. 753-8.

3. 7.8-18.

4. *Persians* 93-114.

5. *Trojan Women* 1053-9 for the decision; 1100-17 for the assumption that Helen is quite safe in the hands of Menelaus.

6. 687-8.

7. I use these terms as convenient labels for general types of story, and insofar as I do use them, the terms are not meant to be exclusive. Though

the *Electra* of Sophocles, for instance, is a revenge-play of the purest possible type, it is also a discovery-play or truth-action. But the presence of Orestes, supposed dead (as in a foundling-story) is not, like the revenge, essential to the plot of an *Electra*. Euripides does without the supposed death altogether.

8. The original plan is to kill Jason, his bride, and her father, *Medea* 375. The plan to murder the children is first formed after the interview with Aegeus, and as a necessary part of the general scheme for revenge 791–3; and the decision is weighed, almost abandoned, then reconfirmed in the long monologue, 1019–80.

9. Iliad 16.431–61; for reconsideration of the fate of Hector, see 22.167–87; of Troy itself, 4.1–72.

10. 205–16.

11. 1374–8.

12. 943.

13. 944–57.

14. Introduction to Denniston and Page, *Agamemnon*, pp. xx–xxvii.

15. *Agamemnon* 205–27.

16. *Agamemnon* 218: ἐπεὶ δ'ἀνάγκας ἔδυ λέπαδνον. The verb ἔδυ is at least active. I have here altered my published translation.

17. *Republic* 10.617d–e.

18. *Agamemnon* 247–8.

19. Note on the passage just quoted.

20. *Pythian* 11.22–3. The Scholia attest two victories for Thrasydaeus, the hero of the ode, one in 474 B.C. and one in 454. The Scholiasts themselves and most scholars have favored the earlier date, but the later cannot be ruled out of consideration. If 454 is right, Pindar probably knew the work of Aeschylus.

21. See *Cypria*, p. 495 Evelyn-White; Hesiod, *Catalogue*, p. 205 Evelyn-White (=Pausanias 1.43.1). For Iphigeneia among the Taurians, Herodotus 4.103. On the whole subject, see Preller-Robert vol. 2, pp. 1095–6, and in particular 1096–8, making it evident that the substituted animal is as a regular feature of the story.

22. *Poetics* 17.5–9: "The stories, whether they are traditional or whether you make them up yourself, should first be sketched in outline and then expanded by putting in episodes. I mean that one might look at the general outline, say of the *Iphigeneia*, like this: A certain maiden has been sacrificed, and has disappeared beyond the ken of those who

sacrificed her and has been established in another country, etc." (Hamilton Fyfe's translation.)

23. See above, pp. 32-4.

24. See above, pp. 37-8.

25. Aeschylus, *Seven* 689-91.

26. Sophocles, *Oedipus Tyrannus* 1169-70.

27. The ending of Euripides, *Iphigeneia in Aulis* is admittedly spurious as it stands in the ms., but Aelian, *Historia Animalium* 7.39, has quoted two and a half lines from what must have been the original ending, running thus:

> I will put a horned doe in the Achaians' hands which they will sacrifice and sacrificing think it is your daughter.

As has been recognized since Porson, this must be Artemis as *deux ex machina* speaking to Clytaemestra. If so, it may be conjectured that, for some reason, secrecy was enjoined upon Clytaemestra and the Chorus, compare the end of Euripides, *Ion* (1601-2).

In Euripides, *Alcestis,* the choice, once made, is adhered to, but its consequences are undone by a miracle, and a miracle (or a trick?) undoes the choice of Sophocles' *Philoctetes,* see text just below.

28. Euripides, *Ion* 1437-8. Ion's first acknowledgment of Creusa's identity is:

> O mother, dearest mother, now I press your face.
> Joy for us both!

29. Sophocles, *Ajax* 1370-3 (Agamemnon to Odysseus):

> Understand me well. I am willing
> to give you this favor and more than this.
> But I will hate this man, alive or dead.
> You may do with him as you please.

30. Euripides, *Heracles* 1246-54; 1347-51.

31. For the legend, see Proclus's summary of *The Cypria,* p. 494 Evelyn-White; of *The Little Iliad,* pp. 508-10; Pausanias 10.27:1; in general, Preller-Robert 2, pp. 1207-18. In his single notice of Philoctetes in *The Iliad* (2.716-27), Homer shows full awareness of his story, but does not develop it. Not only does the story of Philoctetes fall outside the action of *The Iliad,* but Philoctetes has the makings of a hero whose talents and exploits could somewhat dim the lustre of Achilles. Both are necessary men, unjustly treated, lying out of the action (*Iliad*

2.688, 721), to be propitiated by an embassy of heroes, glorious on their final return. If Achilles is heir to the great spear of Peleus, Philoctetes is lord of the still greater bow of Heracles. Achilles slays Hector, but Philoctetes kills Paris, who may well, before Homer, have been the chief warrior of Troy (see e.g., Scott, *The Unity of Homer,* pp. 226-33). The career of neither Hector nor Achilles affected the outcome of the Trojan War, but when Philoctetes killed Paris, Troy fell.

32. In addition to the three great tragic poets, the title is attested for Achaeus, Antiphon, Philocles, and Theodectes. Dio Chrysostom, *Oration* 52, has left a comparison, with all too little detail, of the versions by the three great poets; in *Oration* 59, he gives a prose version of the prologue to the lost tragedy of Euripides. For the lost *Philoctetes at Troy* of Sophocles, see Fragments 635-40.

33. Dio, *Oration* 59.4; Plutarch, *Moralia* 1108b; and see Jebb, Introduction to Sophocles, *Philoctetes,* pp. xviii-xxi.

34. Sophocles, *Philoctetes* 120. Neoptolemus then proceeds to display a good deal more proficiency as a liar than we might have expected, but the dramatic story demands that Philoctetes shall be convincingly deceived at the outset.

35. I have no hope that this heretical thought will be seriously entertained by many. It is not, of course, a question of what "really happened," only of what Sophocles might have had in mind. How can we ever know that? I note only these points. First, the actor who played the part was, in a very real sense (like the Merchant in an earlier scene) Odysseus in disguise. Second, the self-introduction of Heracles, 1411-12:

φάσκειν δ'αὐδὴν τὴν Ἡρακλέους
ἀκοῆ τε κλύειν λεύσσειν τ'ὄψιν

is curiously irresolute or tentative, though it gets some support from *Electra* 9. Finally, if this is in truth Heracles, it is the only case I know of where, in a situation of intrigue, Odysseus is left baffled and defeated, without another ace up his sleeve.

36. 902-3.

37. 908, and see also 895, 969, 974 (Neoptolemus); 963 (Chorus); 949, 1063, 1350 (Philoctetes).

38. To judge by the title and the contents of Euripides' play. Aeschylus's Fragments (74-7) tell us nothing about the action.

39. Sophocles, *Antigone* 904-28.

40. Thucydides, 1.2, 5-6.

41. In the trilogy by Aeschylus which opened with *The Suppliant Maidens,* a victory of the Egyptians must almost necessarily be inferred.

42. In *The Heracleidae,* the voluntary death of Macaria and the death-sentence on Eurystheus; in *The Suppliant Women* the character-sketch of the seven against Thebes and the episode of Euadne's suicide.

43. In *The Phoenician Women* of Euripides, the victim is a young man, Menoeceus, but the fact that he is unmarried, not even engaged, is emphasized 944–8.

44. For *Erechtheus,* see Euripides, Fragments 349–70, but I do not find any reference to a choice by the daughter. Since Euripides in the play spoke of the transformation of Erechtheus's three daughters into the Hyades, one may suppose that, as in *Iphigeneia in Aulis,* there was a last-minute rescue or apotheosis.

45. Fragment 360. The speech is quoted at length (55 lines) by Lycurgus, *Against Leocrates* 100.

46. Sophocles, Fragments 122–35; Euripides, Fragments 114–56. The virgin-sacrifice here is combined with the pride-and-punishment story, Andromeda's mother, Cassiopeia, had offended by rivalling the Nereids in beauty. Eratosthenes, *Catasterism* 16. See Nauck on Sophocles, Fragment 122.

47. Sophocles, Fragments 479–85 Nauck, 522–8 Pearson, with his prefatory note.

48. There is no choice for Iphigeneia in Aeschylus, *Agamemnon* 228–49, but here she is not a heroine in action but an image in a flashback.

49. *Agamemnon* 239–42; Euripides, *Iphigeneia in Aulis* 613–16 (fragility at least, but this is also Clytaemestra's *grande dame* manner); Polyxena, Euripides, *Hecuba* 557–61, repeating *Agamemnon,* loc. cit., in more explicit detail.

50. *Hymn to Demeter* 1–21.

51. Sophocles, *Antigone* 810–16; 876–8; 1240–1, with perhaps also 781–801; see Goheen, *The Imagery of Sophocles' Antigone,* pp. 37–41. Compare also the sixth-century epitaph, Kaibel, *Epigrammata Graeca* 6.

52. Herodotus 7.220–1. One thinks of the semi-legendary king of Athens, Codrus (for material see Scherling in *RE* s.v. Kodros) who died for Athens. Dated four generations after Nestor, he must have been thought by the tragic poets—if indeed they knew the story at all—to be too late and "historical" for tragedy, as there is no trace of him in the tragic corpus. Plato, however, seems to have known the story,

Symposium 208d, where he is mentioned along with Alcestis and Achilles, see below, note 55.

53. *Iliad* 2.701–2; Proclus's summary of *The Cypria,* p. 495 Evelyn-White. For Sophocles, *Poemenes (The Herdsmen),* see fragments 497–521 Pearson, with his notes; for Euripides, *Protesilaus,* fragments 647–57 Nauck.

54. For Euadne, Euripides, *The Suppliant Women* 980–1113; for the fragments of *Protesilaus,* see last note, also Hyginus 103–4 for the story probably followed by Euripides. Laodameia caressed a statue of her husband, as Admetus promised to take a statue of Alcestis to bed with him, *Alcestis* 348–54. See Aeschylus, *Agamemnon* 414–19.

55. The "Achilles tetralogy" of Aeschylus doubtless included *The Myrmidons, The Nereids,* and *The Phrygians* or *The Ransoming of Hector.* See Smyth, *Aeschylus,* vol. 2, p. 378, and the fragments in his collection under the plays named. According to Plato, Aeschylus made Achilles the lover of Patroclus, *Symposium* 180 a–b, see also 208d, and for confirmation three lines from *The Myrmidons,* fragments 64, 65 Smyth. In Homer, *Iliad* 18.95–100, Achilles is ready to avenge Patroclus though he knows or understands that his own death will follow; which, despite Plato, is not quite the same thing as unconditional unwillingness to go on living.

56. Pindar, *Pythia* 11.22–3.

57. 35–7.

58. 1505–7.

59. Aeschylus, *The Libation Bearers* 1068–76.

60. Introduction to *The Bacchae,* p. xliii.

61. For the story, see Apollodorus, *Library* 2.4.1–3; Hyginus 63; these probably represent the general plot of Euripides, *Dictys,* fragments 331–48.

62. For extensive fragments of Euripides, *Antiope,* see Page, *Greek Literary Papyri,* pp. 60–71, in addition to fragments 179–227 in Nauck; and for the story, Hyginus 8; Apollodorus, *Library* 3.5.5.

63. See above, pp. 40–1.

64. For the tokens, Euripides, *Iphigeneia in Tauris* 808–26.

65. See, e.g., Platnauer, Introduction to Euripides, *Iphigeneia in Tauris,* pp. xv-xvii.

66. Euripides, *Helen* 241–51, compare *Homeric Hymn to Demeter* 1–21, also Euripides, *Ion* 887–96. For the faint legend of the sacrifice of Helen,

like Iphigeneia's miraculously intercepted, see Preller-Robert 2, pp. 338–9.

67. *Helen* 1301–68.

68. E.g., Sophocles, *Ajax* 693–718; *Antigone* 1115–54; *Women of Trachis* 633–82; Euripides, *Heracles* 734–814, compare *Trojan Women* 701–5.

69. Sophocles, *Oedipus Tyrannus* 883–910; 945–72; Euripides, *Helen* 589–96 (up until this point, our text shows illusion played against reality on every page).

70. Bacchylides 5.56–154, see the material assembled by Pearson on the fragments of Sophocles, *Meleager*; Preller-Robert 2, pp. 88–100. Euripides also wrote a *Meleager*, fragments 515–39, as did Antiphon and Sosiphanes.

71. Bacchylides 15; Sophocles, *Women of Trachis*; Preller-Robert 2, pp. 567–601.

72. For the sword of Hector, Sophocles, *Ajax* 815–18; for the fatal spot, Aeschylus, fragment 83; for variants, *Hypothesis* to Sophocles, *Ajax*. I omit the fatal heel or foot of Achilles, since it is not attested early, except perhaps on a sixth-century vase from Chalkis, where the body of Achilles is shown lying transfixed through the ankle. In Plato, *Symposium* 219e it is Ajax, not Achilles, who is called ἄτρωτος σιδήρῳ. See Preller-Robert 2, pp. 67–8.

73. See the material assembled by Pearson on the fragments of Sophocles, *Odysseus Acanthoplex*.

74. *Iliad* 9.524–8; Bacchylides 5.63–92.

75. *Iliad* 2.768–9; 13.321–5; Pindar, *Nemea* 7.27–30; Sophocles, *Ajax* 418–27.

76. See for instance *Odyssey* 1.163–5.

77. Even for Hector, there is a hint that he fails because he is wearing the wrong armor, *Iliad* 17.188–208; 22.321–7. Did its magic once work in reverse against the wrong master? But Homer prefers to have him fall to a greater man more greatly favored and better armed.

78. Vergil, *Aeneid* 1.474–5. The phrase is applied to Troilus, not Hector, but it could apply to Hector.

79. See Whitman, *Sophocles* 59–60.

80. Sophocles, *Women of Trachis* 1143–5.

81. *Iliad* 18.117–19, compare Euripides, *Alcestis* 989–90; *Inscriptiones Graecae* 12.2.384.7–8.

IV. CHARACTER, IMAGERY, RHETORIC, CEREMONY

1. One must here distinguish between such well "documented" figures and characters who are merely identified in legend but who in drama are made to develop considerable personality; such as Creon and Haemon, Chrysothemis, Phaedra, Rhesus, perhaps Pylades. Scholars and critics tend to over-interpret character, to ferret out details of personality which are simply not there. See Dale, Introduction to Euripides, *Alcestis*, pp. xxii-xxix; Waldock, *Sophocles,* pp. 11–24. Such lonely and salutary warnings should be read again and again. But we must still qualify our restraints in view of the legendary-historical fulness of certain characters used in drama and fiction. Tolstoi's Pierre and Andrei have, as Waldock would say, only the dimensions given them by Tolstoi, but his Napoleon has also those given by history. Nor was the creator of Odysseus in *Ajax* and *Philoctetes* altogether free from Homer, the *Cycle,* or even Pindar.

2. As we should say, not this kind of story. In Euripides, *Andromache* 1085–165, this is in fact what does happen to Neoptolemus.

3. Sophocles, *The Women of Trachis* 177, 488, 811. See Kitto, *Greek Tragedy,* p. 308.

4. 269–73.

5. Sophocles, *Oedipus Tyrannus* 124, 345, 378, 787, 794, 1062.

6. For instance, when chosen by lot to fight Hector, he boasts of his valor only as one of a whole group of Achaians, *Iliad* 7.226–32. Contrast Sophocles, *Ajax* 421–6.

7. No god specifically aids Ajax in *The Iliad.* In *Ajax* 762–75 he is reported to have dismissed the proffered aid of Athene and by implication all divine aid. This is not attested in epic as we know it.

8. 1058–63.

9. Scholiast on *Apollonius Rhodius* 1.1212; for her warcraft, Apollodorus, *Library* 1.8.2; see Preller-Robert 2.87.

10. Deianeira uses words expressing the idea of fear ($\phi\delta\beta os$, $\tau a\rho\beta\hat{\omega}$, $\delta\epsilon\delta o\iota\kappa a$, etc.) at lines 23–5, 28, 37, 150, 176, 296–7, 307, 457, 550, 630, 663, 666.

11. Apollodorus, *Library* 1.8.2; 9.16.

12. Euripides, *Alcestis* 926–8.

13. *Poetics* 6.13.

14. The limitations of dramatic form are very well illustrated in the

works of Shaw, who is constantly struggling to escape them. Shaw can do "the whole character in a little half-line." He is a master of dramatic technique (and a poor novelist) but he is restless within his form. So we have the full prefaces and epilogues. In *Pygmalion*, he is so afraid of the melodramatic and dramatically logical ending that he tacks on an anti-dramatic unplayable conclusion in case-history form. His plays abound in novelistic description not only of the appearance but of the whole natures of characters. In *The Man of Destiny,* for instance, we begin with five full pages of "Stage direction." Some two hundred words are devoted to the entrance of a secondary character, including: "He is a chuckle-headed young man of 24, with the fair, delicate, clear skin of a man of rank, and a self-assurance which the French Revolution has failed to shake in the smallest degree. He has a thick silly lip, an eager credulous eye, an obstinate nose, and a loud confident voice. A young man without fear, without reverence, without imagination," etc., etc. One may sometimes wonder what this excellent prose has to do with the theatre, whether Shaw's work can be compared with Greek drama at all.

15. Assuming that each tragic poet in the competition had a day to himself. The alternative would be a major dramatic part on each of three successive days. There is no evidence that I know of.

16. See *Vita* of Sophocles, 6: Aristotle, *Poetics* 9.11.

17. See Dale, Introduction to Euripides, *Alcestis,* pp. xxvii-xxix.

18. *Works and Days* 202-12.

19. 385-6.

20. 885-7; 970-5.

21. Aeschylus, *Prometheus* 1043-53.

22. Euripides, *Medea* 230-51.

23. See for instance Murray, *Ritual Forms in Greek Tragedy,* pp. 343, 354, 359.

24. The whole scenes are *Ajax* 1047-162; 1226-317; *Antigone* 414-525; 635-765; *Alcestis* 614-740.

25. Sophocles, *Antigone* 661-71 on Pearson's arrangement of the text.

26. Plato, *Gorgias* 454-7c.

27. Plato, *Apology* 196.

28. 967-8.

29. Introduction to Euripides, *Alcestis,* p. xxviii.

30. Sophocles, *Oedipus Tyrannus* 583-602; Euripides, *Hippolytus* 1007-20.

31. 522–78.

32. Sophocles, *Antigone* 450–7.

33. *Poetics* 6.5. Here he uses the phrase, ὁ τῆς ὄψεως κόσμος, which would cover not only what I mean here but any orderly visual representation.

34. 10.503–11.234.

35. 31–44.

36. Sophocles, *Oedipus Tyrannus* 1–3; 15–19; 142–50. This kind of ceremony relates to the use of the silent character so beautifully exemplified by Iole in *The Women of Trachis*.

37. Aeschylus, *The Suppliant Maidens* 186–206; 223–5.

38. Sophocles, *Ajax* 1402–17.

39. Sophocles, *Oedipus at Colonus* 466–92.

40. *Oedipus Tyrannus* 911–23.

41. *Electra* 634–59.

42. *Agamemnon* 385. See above, p. 39.

43. Sophocles, *Electra* 1442–80.

44. Euripides, *Alcestis* 1019–36.

45. 1110–19.

46. 305–8; 328–33.

47. 1042–69.

48. Shakespeare, *The Merchant of Venice*, Act 5, Scene 1.

49. *Poetics* 14.18–19.

BIBLIOGRAPHY

PRINCIPAL TEXTS USED

Aeschylus, ed. and tr. H. W. Smyth. London and New York, 2nd printing, 1952. Contains fragments, and appendix ed. and tr. H. Lloyd-Jones.

Aristotle, The Poetics, ed. and tr. W. Hamilton Fyfe. Cambridge, Mass., and London, revised and reprinted 1946.

Euripidis Fabulae, ed. G. Murray, 3 vols. Oxford, 1901–9.

Greek Literary Papyri, ed. and tr. D. L. Page. Cambridge, Mass., and London, 1942.

Sophoclis Fabulae, ed. A. C. Pearson. Oxford, 1923.

The Fragments of Sophocles, ed. A. C. Pearson, 3 vols. Cambridge, 1917.

Tragicorum Graecorum Fragmenta, ed. A. Nauck, 2nd ed. Leipzig, 1926.

OTHER WORKS USED AND CONSULTED

Bowra, C. M. *Greek Lyric Poetry.* Oxford, 1936.

— *Sophoclean Tragedy.* Oxford, 1944.

— *Problems in Greek Poetry.* Oxford, 1953.

Carpenter, R. *Folk Tale, Fiction, and Saga in the Homeric Epics.* Berkeley, 1946.

Dale, A. M. *Euripides: Alcestis.* Oxford, 1954.

Denniston, J. D. and Page, D. L. *Aeschylus: Agamemnon.* Oxford, 1957.

Dodds, E. R. *Euripides: Bacchae.* Oxford, 1944.

— "Euripides the Irrationalist," *Classical Review,* XLIII (1929), 97–104.

Else, G. *Aristotle's Poetics: The Argument.* Cambridge, Mass., 1957.

Evelyn-White, H. G. *Hesiod, the Homeric Hymns and Homerica,* 3rd ed. London and Cambridge, Mass., 1936.

Farnell, L. R. *The Cults of the Greek States. Oxford,* 1896–1909.

Freud, S. *Moses and Monotheism.* Translated by Katherine Jones. New York, 1939.

Goheen, R. F. *The Imagery of Sophocles' Antigone.* Princeton, 1951.

Grande, C. Dél. *Hybris.* Naples, 1947.

Grube, G. M. A. *The Drama of Euripides.* London, 1941.

Harrison, J. E. *Prolegomena to the Study of Greek Religion.* Cambridge, 1903.

— *Themis,* 2nd ed. Cambridge, 1927.

Harry, J. H. *Aeschylus: Prometheus.* New York, Cincinnati, and Chicago, 1905.

Harsh, P. W. *"Ἁμαρτία* Again," *Transactions of the American Philological Association* LXXVI (1945), 47–58.

Jaeger, W. *Paideia I.* Translated by G. Highet. New York, 1945.

Jebb, R. C. *Sophocles.* Cambridge, 1885–1902.

Kitto, H. D. F. *Form and Meaning in Drama.* London, 1956.

— *Greek Tragedy.* Anchor Edition, New York, 1950.

Kranz, W. *Stasimon.* Berlin, 1933.

Lattimore, R. *The Poetry of Greek Tragedy.* Baltimore and Oxford, 1958.

Lehrs, K. *Populäre Aufsätze.* Leipzig, 1856.

Lesky, A. "Das Hellenistische Gyges-Drama." *Hermes,* LXXXI (1953), 1–10.

Lioudaki, M. Στοῦ Πάππου τὰ Γόνατα. Athens, no date.

Lloyd-Jones, H. "Zeus in Aeschylus," *Journal of Hellenic Studies,* LXXVI (1956), 55–67.

Masqueray, P. *Sophocle.* Paris, 1922.

Meyer, E. *Geschichte des Altertums.* Stuttgart and Berlin, 1884–1909.

Murray, G. "Excursus on the Ritual Forms Preserved in Greek Tragedy," in Harrison, *Themis,* 340–63.

Norwood, G. *Essays on Euripidean Drama.* Berkeley, 1954.

Orwell, G. *Dickens, Dali and Others.* New York, 1946.

Page, D. L. *A New Chapter in the History of Greek Tragedy.* Cambridge, 1951.

— *Euripides: Medea.* Oxford, 1938.

Pickard-Cambridge, A. W. *Dithyramb, Tragedy and Comedy.* Oxford, 1927.

— *The Dramatic Festivals of Athens.* Oxford, 1953.

Platnauer, M. *Euripides: Iphigenia in Tauris.* Oxford, 1938.

Pohlenz, M. *Die griechische Tragödie,* 2nd ed. Göttingen, 1954.

Post, L. A. *From Homer to Menander.* Berkeley, 1951.

Preller, L. *Griechische Mythologie,* 4th ed., revised by C. Robert. Berlin, 1894–1926.

Rivier, A. *Essai sur le tragique d'Euripide.* Lausanne, 1944.

Robert, C. *Oidipus.* Berlin, 1915.

Schmid, W. *Geschichte der Griechischen Literatur.* Munich, 1929–48.

Sidgwick, A. *Aeschylus: Agamemnon,* 6th ed. Oxford, 1905.

Thompson, S. *Motif-Index of Folk-Literature, Indiana University Studies,* no. 96, etc. Bloomington, 1932–6.

Waldock, A. J. A. *Sophocles the Dramatist.* Cambridge, 1951.

Webster, T. B. L. *An Introduction to Sophocles.* Oxford, 1936.

Whitman, C. H. *Sophocles.* Cambridge, Mass., 1951.

Wilamowitz-Möllendorff, T. von. *Die dramatische Technik des Sophokles.* Berlin, 1917.

Wilamowitz-Möllendorff, U. von. *Euripides: Herakles,* 1st ed. Berlin, 1889.

INDEX OF PASSAGES

Note: Works which have not survived intact are marked ★. In references to plays the absence of line numbers indicates general discussion of the work named or the discussion of a group of passages not warranting separate mention.